To Cas, Reed, Adrienne, Garrett, and Yvette.
May you find your passion and make your dreams a reality.

CONTENTS

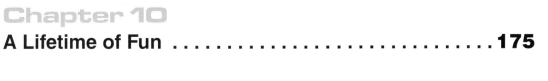

ACKNOWLEDGMENTS

The people who contributed their knowledge, expertise, and coaching skills are what make this book special. The most accomplished, innovative, and respected coaches in the world served as my consultants, advisors, and sounding board in making this project happen. Jay and Anne Bennett of Bennett's Water Ski and Wakeboard School have always been there for me, and so many others opened up their homes and ski sites to us and modeled for great photos that really bring the coaching points to life. Jay and Freddy Krueger (former staff member of Bennett's) contributed to chapter 7, Jump Skiing, as well.

I could not have finished chapter 5, Wakeboarding, without the direction of Mike Ferraro and the editing of Chet Raley. Chet's coaching skills and ideas are also used in a few other chapters. Mike Ferraro shaped how I wrote this book. He also urged me to contact Brent Larson, who spent hours with me not only on writing chapter 6, Trick Skiing, but also on helping me explain some concepts that are shaping how athletes train, move, and compete. Brent connected me with Harold Harb, innovator of snow ski coaching. Harold's ideas and ability to explain the movements of our sport changed how I ski, train, and coach. Harold and Brent's contributions were incredibly helpful in chapter 3, Fundamental Movements and Boat Motion. Although I am a slalom skier, the insights of Steven Schnitzer, Andy Mapple, and Mark Bozicevic make that chapter one that I turn to when I get lost and am trying to figure out how to get a few extra buoys or set up my ski.

Skiing is a team sport no matter who is behind the boat or on the podium. You need a family to support you and allow you to pursue your dreams. My wife, Yvette, and kids, Cas, Reed, Adrienne, and Garrett, have provided the opportunity and have sacrificed so I can chase my dreams and accomplish my goals. I am eternally grateful. You need a driver and ski partners to train and motivate you. I have a great one: Matt Heinz. There are many others I ski with, not as often as Matt, who always help me in more ways than they might understand. They keep the process of improvement as fun as the results. Thank you, John, Marc, Marco, Doug, Jerome, Steve, Kyle, Chad, and Boz.

Similarly, publishing a book is a team sport. Justin, Heather, and Neil, thank you for making it happen on the publishing side. Thanks to Dave Goode for providing skis and Chuck Gleason for providing Eagle vests and gear. And a final huge thank-you to all of the skiers and Bennett's pro staff members who helped out in so many ways: Andy, Steve, Matteo, Megan, Esteban, Alvaro, Ramona, Stinne, Chris, Daniel, Claire, David, and Ace.

When you drive by or fly over a body of water, do you wonder who's riding on that lake and whether a slider, jump, or slalom course could fit in it? Have you found yourself waking up at 6 a.m. to get the smooth-as-glass water, going to coaches and camps, and spending hours chatting it up with fellow addicts about the best techniques, skis, boards, bindings, boats, drivers, coaches, and lakes? If so, you're not alone in your craving to get more of those ever-elusive, adrenaline-packed moments when you feel at one with your ski(s) or board, effortlessly linking turns or tricks and rocketing off a jump. At last count, over 11 million people in the United States, and double that worldwide, share your passion for water skiing or wakeboarding.

Skiers and wakeboarders are long on ambition and die-hard in their resolve, but many, even some of the best-known pros, train haphazardly at best. Many are tempted to do what others are doing without recognizing that they may have a completely different style and struggle with completely different issues of technique, style, or equipment.

This book will arm you with the facts, based on research, about what to do on and off the water. It also offers a process, framework, and vocabulary to guide you in getting better where it matters, behind the boat. When you buy a new boat, you get an owner's manual to teach you how to safely operate and maintain your new toy. This book is like an owner's manual that will teach you how to safely achieve your own best performance behind the boat.

Need for Continuous Improvement

Kaizen is a Japanese philosophy that focuses on continuous improvement throughout all aspects of life. Simply put, the idea is to find and fix the flaw, which improves the system.

How does this apply to skiing or wakeboarding? Many boarders' and skiers' process of learning and getting better is erratic and inconsistent. Often, people improve rapidly at first, but as the moves, tricks, and techniques get more difficult, fundamental weaknesses prevent them from getting better. They may lack the necessary strength and conditioning; they may not have the right skis, board, bindings, gloves, or boat; they may not understand the proper technique; or they may not have the mental discipline to stick with the process of improvement. In many cases, skill development plateaus and frustration sets in, sometimes reducing the fun, too. The good news is that you can improve and perform better.

No matter how much you know or how good you are, you can always improve some facet of your skills. Many athletes raising the championship trophy or receiving the gold metal are tremendously skilled and may well be the best their sport has ever seen, but have not yet realized their full potential. To be as good as you can be, you need a systematic way to assess yourself, find problems, and make improvements.

Process for Continuous Improvement

The USA Water Ski coaches' manual says: "Technically speaking, water skiing is a highly sophisticated and complex outcome based movement task that requires the skier to perceive, interpret, and perform a variety of movement combinations with accuracy, finesse, timing, and power. A skillful performance in water skiing is the result of developing the awareness and perception required to interpret environmental factors such as wind and water conditions in combination with assessing the performance of equipment and determining the skill movement that will be best suited for the situation." Although this may sound daunting, the process for improvement is not.

In his 2000 book, *Ambition,* sociologist Gilbert Brim discussed how humans seem to be most happy and motivated when faced with what he called "manageable difficulties"—challenges that are neither too easy (because then we become bored) nor too hard (because then we become discouraged). What we need is a learning system that builds on success, continually challenges us, and pushes us in new and different ways so we can manage success and failure as we strive to be better.

I use a skill improvement system called the 25 percent rule. It states that your potential is equal to the sum of your ability in each of four components of skiing or wakeboarding: equipment selection and fitting, strength and conditioning, technique and skill development, and competition. You reach your ultimate potential only when all four components are working together, totaling 100 percent peak performance.

The first step in applying the 25 percent rule is to select an athlete to emulate for each component. You can use a different athlete for each component, but try to make it someone who skis or boards in a way you would like to. Anyone who has watched slalom legends Andy Mapple and Kris LaPoint may notice that they carry speed and turn as though they were on a railroad track, staying in the water in any conditions and staying at a consistent angle, making their skiing aggressive, smooth, and predictable. Both Andy and Kris have spent years perfecting their equipment and ski setups. For strength and conditioning, few skiers can compare to Jamie Beauchesne or Chris Parrish. The strength-to-weight ratios of these two are off the charts. You can put Freddy Krueger into that mix as a jumper.

When choosing someone to emulate for technique, consider two factors: your personal style and your body type. Although you may be in awe of Darin Shapiro's style and moves on the water, if your body type and natural movement style are more like Jeremy Kovak's, you would want to emulate him.

In terms of knowing how to win, few are better than Jodi Fisher. He understands how to adjust to all types of conditions, and most important, he has mastered the skill of winning and performing his best in the clutch. This makes him an ideal model of competition toughness.

The next step in the 25 percent rule is to rate yourself on a scale of 1 to 25 in each of the four components. You may want to ask a coach or training partner to assess your skills to see whether your evaluation is consistent with what others see. If you are comparing yourself to a top pro rider, rate that person a 25 in his or her area.

The next step of the 25 percent rule involves assessing your results and prioritizing your training by focusing on your area of weakness. If, for example, your strength and conditioning has really suffered over the last year, you may want to spend more time in the gym and less time at the dining establishments during the off-season. Write down three actions you can take and when you are going to take them to raise your skill level 3 to 5 points on the 25-point scale. As your most glaring areas of weakness improve, usually you will find that other areas improve as well. Listing only three actions helps you stay focused and not be overwhelmed by everything you need to work on.

Whether you are concerned with your technique and skill development, strength and conditioning, equipment fitting and setup, or competition toughness, the systematic approach of the 25 percent rule can ensure success, constant skill improvement, and enjoyment.

Like the 25 percent rule, this book is set up as a series of small steps, or learning progressions. It begins at the water, first focusing on your board, skis, and bindings and getting you into equipment that will fit your skill level and body type. Next, the book focuses on the strength and conditioning required to perform on the water. Following is an in-depth look at the basic movements of the sport, which are then incorporated into learning progressions for each event. Once you are ready, the book prepares you for competition by addressing mental toughness and strategies for doing your best and bringing home the gold. The book also includes some information on how to get the most out of the sport at any age so you can train with more enjoyment and fewer frustrations for years to come.

Chapter 1

Skiing and Wakeboarding Equipment

Nothing can accelerate the improvement of skills faster than using the right equipment on the water. All of your equipment, from your board or skis to your bindings to your rope, gloves, and handle, must fit your skill level, body type, and riding style. At every clinic I teach and tournament I go to, the majority of the participants (pros, too) are on skis and boards that do not fit them in some manner or are set up incorrectly. Sadly, these athletes are out there giving their all, not realizing that their equipment is the culprit in many of their performance problems.

The wrong equipment not only holds you back from achieving your goals and deprives you of the satisfaction of doing your best, but also can make performing some moves difficult or even impossible. Worse yet, having the wrong equipment can cause injuries. I can attest to both. I have experienced frustration, self-doubt, and injuries as a result of having the wrong equipment or setup. These problems have cost me victories and records as well as physical pain. Conversely, I have experienced the rush and confidence of having my ski tuned perfectly, bindings fitting just right for maximum comfort and control, and handle and gloves just right to allow me to put a death grip on the 380-horsepower beast slinging me across the course. Your enjoyment, safety, and success on the water all begin with getting the right equipment. *Nothing* is more important in setting the stage for your success and constant improvement.

Equipment Selection and Fitting

Over the last decade, the Water Sports Industry Association has seen a true revolution of performance-enhancing innovation in every aspect of the equipment used on the water. The changes in shapes, materials, and designs have made the sport easier to learn, attracting hundreds of new boarders and skiers to the water. Additionally, professional performances continue to improve, and world records keep falling. Equipment purchased just a year or two ago (skis, boards, bindings, ropes) is already outdated. Upgrading to modern technology will yield results that will astound you.

Like most skiers and boarders, you probably love going out to buy the latest and greatest equipment. Few things are more exciting than that first ride on a new ski or that first launch off the wake on a new board. Before you place that order, though, remember one word: *you*. Buy the equipment that fits you—your style, your weight, your height, your ability, and your needs. Notice I did not say your wants, your color preference, your graphic choice, your favorite skiers' choice, or your salesperson's choice. This chapter will help you filter out the hype and fluff and ask the right questions so you will have the equipment you need to perform at your best and keep getting better.

Bindings

The logical place to begin a discussion on equipment is at the point most critical to keeping you on your skis or board: your bindings. You need bindings that will give you optimal alignment on your skis or board. Being optimally aligned from your feet up minimizes the effort you need to balance and control your movement on the skis or board and stacks your bones and muscles to maximize strength and reduce stress on your joints. This gives you the best feel, or sense, of what your board or skis are doing and how you need to move to get them in correct positions.

When you stand in your bindings with your feet about hip-width apart, your hips, knees, and feet should be aligned with each other, as shown in figure 1.1. This will make skiing or boarding more comfortable, more enjoyable, and easier to start. The next step is to achieve optimal stability. You want a dynamically effective foot bed that puts as much of the foot's surface as possible in direct contact with the skis or board. Adjustments in alignment and stability can then be tuned by installing shim strips under your bindings. As an example, I have about a 2-centimeter shim under the left back heel of my foot bed because of lost flexion in that ankle due to an injury and surgery. This shim allows me to flex and align so I can maintain fore–aft balance on the ski.

Figure 1.1 **Proper adjustment of the bindings and skis keeps the hips, knees, and feet in alignment.**

Your next decision is whether to choose a rubber or a hard-shell binding. Although hard-shell bindings are now used by the overwhelming majority of top slalom and trick skiers, jumpers and boarders have not adopted them to the same degree. For slalom and tricks, hard-shell bindings provide three performance advantages:

○ **Comfort.** If you suffer from cramped feet as a result of poorly fitting bindings, you will definitely benefit from hard-shell bindings. You can ski as long as your hands can hold out with hard-shells. Extra passes means more time on the water and faster improvement.

Finding Your Foot Bed

The foot beds of most off-the-shelf bindings provide too much cushion to be adequate. The softness of the material allows your foot to move around in the binding, which prevents the most effective transmission of your leg movements to the skis or board. Many top skiers and boarders use custom foot beds that result in a more responsive ride. These foot beds can be expensive (anywhere from $40 to over $200), but they are a great investment. If you opt for customized foot beds, be sure to talk to a good snow ski shop. These shops fit snow skier's boots all the time and have a great understanding of the fit that's required. Some off-the-shelf moldable materials are available, but these may not result in proper support, alignment, or stability of the foot either. Machines that produce instant insoles may also be available, but they too may not put the foot in a balanced configuration. Taking the time to find the right system is essential and may require visiting an orthotic professional to ensure that you get the most for your money and a good fit for performance and comfort.

○ **Ski edging and tipping control.** A hard-shell binding fixes the ankle in a flexed position. As a result, you cannot control the skis with ankle and foot movements. Instead, you have to use your hips and knees to edge the skis. This is beneficial because the foot and ankle are made up of hundreds of small bones and muscles that are hard to control at high speeds. By moving the control point farther up on the leg, you use bigger and stronger bones and muscles to control the skis. The result is a dramatic improvement in edge control and leverage of the skis. Adopting a hard-shell binding will require an adjustment period. You may need a set or two to relearn how to edge and turn the skis, but the performance benefit is well worth the time. I have seen top skiers and students alike make drastic improvements in body position and ski control as well as in their scores using hard-shell systems.

○ **Safety.** Although hard-shell bindings do provide better support and protection for the foot and ankle, questions always arise regarding the release system. How do you detach the bindings from the skis or board after a fall? Manufacturers provide a variety of release systems including industrial Velcro systems, modified snow ski systems, and permanent fixture systems that do not detach from the ski. The best choice is whichever system you like the most. With hard-shell systems, you get to choose how much force causes the release of your skis, whereas your foot may simply slip out of a rubber binding.

Regardless of the type of binding you use, you need to focus on lateral support and alignment and how your knees track in the bindings. Tracking happens when you flex your knees and they move forward over your bindings. Ideally, your knee should track in a straight line along the center of the foot, moving over your second toe. If your knees come closer together because they track inward, your legs may twist when on the water, which can result in skidding or sliding of the skis or board or less edge control, making carving or turning more difficult. Tracking to the outside causes fewer problems, but it can affect your balance. The essential element you are looking for is a lateral and horizontal stiffness that responsively transmits your edging efforts directly to the skis or board. Boots that twist and rotate generally transmit twisting to the skis while you are trying to edge, making balance and control more difficult. Solid, consistent support results in good performances for most skiers and boarders; unregulated rotary twisting rarely results in good performances.

Fore–aft balance is as important as, and in some events more important than, lateral alignment. Fore–aft boot adjustments are used to match the balance needs of the diverse body types of skiers. Shims and foot bed adjustments can aid fore-aft balance. Like most dynamic movement sports, proper footwork controls balance. Good balance results in good movements. Your foot work on the water is controlled by how well you can move and control your ski or board. For these reasons, you need to always begin fine-tuning your ski or board set up with your bindings before you adjust anything else.

Skis

Finding the skis that fit you correctly and will improve your ability takes more analysis than reading ski test results or online message boards, looking through manufacturers' literature, or comparing prices in mail order catalogs. If you are really serious about trying to improving your skills, you will need to put in some research and testing time. The upside is that getting on the right skis often can mean better performance on the high end and more consistency overall.

The secret to buying skis that will improve your skiing and be more fun to ride is finding those that will help you overcome or eliminate your weaknesses without hampering your strengths. Grab a pen and paper, make four columns, and label them *technical strengths, style strengths, technical weaknesses,* and *style weaknesses.* Ask yourself, *What do I do that makes me a good skier?* Consider whether you have awesome turns, great balance or rotation, or a solid body position. Ask yourself, *What can I count on to bail me out of trouble?* Possibilities may include good knee bend or handle control. Try to identify the qualities you don't have to think about, those that just happen for you when you need them. Now list your weaknesses. Ask yourself, *What do I have to practice and remember to do? What do I constantly need work on? When do I fall the most? Where do I get in trouble?*

With a better understanding of your skiing style, you can look for skis with characteristics that will help you improve in the areas in which you need the most help. This is where the ski test results and message boards can come in handy. The basic idea is to find skis that will improve your strengths and help counteract your weaknesses. For example, if you have determined that you need a slalom ski that will help you get across the course faster, look for skis with stiffness and acceleration. If you need better control and tighter turns, look for soft, more forgiving skis. And remember, at this stage you still are not buying skis; you are merely determining which ones are best suited for you. The real test comes next—when you take a few for a ride.

If you don't demo skis, you won't know whether they will help you, whether they will fit your style, and whether you can get them to work. Take the time, spend the money (pro shops often have a demo fee), and ride three different pairs of skis that you have determined from your strength and weakness analysis will help you the most. Then use the following tips to help you choose.

- **Be patient.** It is extremely rare to hop on a pair of skis and ski your best or anywhere near it. So give every pair a chance—two or three sets, minimum. If you do hop on skis and tear it up, make sure that the skis are doing what they are supposed to do. Be sure they are improving your weaknesses, not merely repeating your performance on the skis you have been riding for years.

- **Make adjustments.** Don't be afraid to make minor adjustments to the bindings and find. The manufacturer has most likely gotten the setup fairly close, so the adjustments should be relatively small (drilling new binding holes would be going too far). Trust your feel and intuition. If you believe you need to make an adjustment, don't hesitate. If you need to slow down quicker, add a bit more wing, and move the fin deeper if you are unstable. Be sure to keep track of your adjustments and their effects in a notebook so you can compare them and find your ideal setting.

- **Forget brand loyalty and graphics.** The equipment manufacturers spend a lot of money coming up with the newest, hottest graphics and even more developing brand loyalty, but the fact is that neither graphics nor loyalty to a ski has ever won a tournament. The top skiers do whatever it takes to their skis to get them to perform their best, and they go through numerous skis to find that ideal setup. You should spend your time finding a pair that works best for you—not those that looks best in the case or are made by the company that made the skis you used to ski on.

○ **Choose the right size and speed.** This seems almost too simple to mention, but I can't tell you how many people I see skiing (the better word may be *struggling*) on skis that are either too big or small for their body type. When I ask people about their skis, the excuses abound. *I have skied on them for years and love it.* (Translation: *I'm too cheap to buy skis that will help my skiing and be more fun to ride.*) *I like this ski because it's so stable.* (Translation: *I'm scared to try a new ski because I might fall a few times.*) My personal favorite came from a 200-pound (91 kg) guy who insisted, "I have always skied on a 65 slalom ski, and I will never be able to turn a 68." (Translation: *I don't want to admit I have gained weight and gotten five years older.*) The fact is that most skiers would benefit from bigger skis. They are more stable, more forgiving, smoother to ride, and less tiring. Bigger skis are especially good for those who ski at slower speeds. This is because bigger skies offer greater acceleration, more consistent turns, and more leverage against the boat.

Combo Pairs

A nice set of combos is a must-have for anyone with a boat. These are basic skis that are most often used to learn how to ski but have evolved into freestyle skis that are a blast to cut, edge, jump, slide, or try just about anything on. These skis are constructed of wood or fiberglass and have flat or slightly concave bottoms with tapered sides (see figure 1.2). The size depends on your weight and the speed you want to ski at. The lighter you are, the smaller your skis should be. Shorter, wider skis are ideally suited for freestyling, but in general, adults over 150 pounds (68 kg) usually use 60- to 70-inch (152 to 178 cm) skis, and children ski on 40- to 50-inch (102 to 127 cm) skis. Additionally, the slower you prefer to ski, the larger your skis should be to reduce drag and body fatigue.

Your best bet is to spend the extra money and buy a nice fiberglass combo pair with a concave bottom and good-fitting bindings. Fiberglass will last much longer than combo pairs made from wood, and the bindings will have less

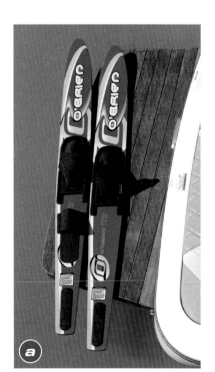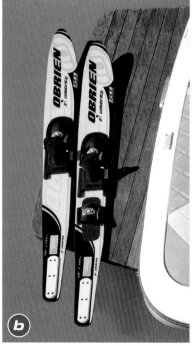

Figure 1.2 Combo pair skis in both *(a)* adult and *(b)* junior sizes are good for learning how to ski.

chance of ripping as a result of dry rotting. Combo skis have adjustable bindings, and you should choose bindings that will come off easily during falls but are well constructed of rubber or another soft synthetic that provides a snug fit with adequate support. Another big benefit of a better combo pair is the slalom ski portion of the pair. This ski has many of the same design features as performance slalom skis but with slight modifications to make it easier to get up on and learn to make smooth, controlled turns. Money spent on a good combo pair is well spent given the durability and wide range of skiability such a pair offers.

Slalom Skis

In 1994, the world's first carbon fiber water ski was introduced, and it changed slalom skiing forever. Tricks, jumping, and wakeboarding soon followed. The acceleration, speed, and reduced weight have made carbon fiber a standard for many high-end skis and boards with great results. All world champions and world record holders have been riding carbon fiber slalom skis. Does that mean you need to run out and buy a carbon fiber slalom ski? Maybe.

Manufacturers want to match you with the perfect ski as badly as you do because they know that if you ski well on it and ski the style the ski is designed for, you will buy more of their skis for years to come. What makes finding the right slalom interesting is that no two skiers are identical, nor are two slalom skis. On top of that, each manufacturer offers three or four models at a variety of price points. How are we to make sense of it?

The secrets to choosing the right slalom ski are not to let your ego or an ignorant salesperson get in the way of getting the right ski for you, and testing skis before making the investment. Select the right ski and you will be off having the best time of your life cutting up the lake rather than fighting the frustrations of falls and body-straining starts. Refer to table 1.1 to determine the correct size ski for you.

TABLE 1.1 **Slalom Ski Size Chart**

	Boat speed (miles per hour)					
	26	28	30	32	34	36
Skier's weight (pounds)	(ski size in inches)					
100	64	64	64	64	64	64
100-115	66	66	66	64	64	64
115-130	67/68	66	66	66	66	66
130-145	67/68	67/68	66	66	66	66
145-160	67/68	67/68	66	66	66	66
160-175	67/68	67/68	67/68	66	66	66/67
175-190	69/70	69/70	67/68	67/68	67/68	66/68
190-205	69/70	69/70	69/70	67/68	67/68	67/68
205-220	69/70	69/70	69/70	69/70	67/68	67/68
220+	69/70	69/70	69/70	69/70	69/70	69/70

Note: If you are on the borderline between sizes, select the larger size ski.

Skiers at all ability levels should look for several things in a slalom ski to make sure it matches their skiing style.

- **Bottom design.** A good slalom ski has a concave bottom that acts like an upside-down airplane wing sucking the ski to the water. This suction allows the ski to hold angle through the pull and helps the ski track (control of the ski when on edge) better in the turn.
- **Beveled edges.** This is the part of the ski that you are riding on during the turn and the part of the ski that you tip or edge with. The width and sharpness of the top and bottom edges dictate the tuning characteristics of the ski. (Refer to chapter 4 for more information about tuning the edges.)
- **Rocker.** The rocker is the curve of the ski from tip to tail. The greater the rocker is, the more the ski will turn, but the less it will accelerate. The opposite is true for a flatter ski.
- **Flex.** The stiffer the ski is, the more difficult it is to turn, but the better it accelerates; the opposite is true for a soft ski. A combination of rocker and flex is critical to dialing a ski in to your style. (See chapter 4 for more information.)

The bindings for slalom skis should fit snugly and comfortably. In slalom, you can choose double boots or a rear toe piece (see figure 1.3). There are advantages to both setups. Let personal preference and comfort guide you, but generally speaking, double boots offer the greatest support and secure fit, but also cost the most; a rear toe piece is easier to get up in and get out of, but does not give you as good a feel for the ski. In both configurations, a slight lift of 1/4 to 1/2 inch (0.6 to 1.3 cm) under your rear heel will help with fore–aft balance and leg flexion and extension movements.

Figure 1.3 Slalom ski binding options include *(a)* double boots and *(b)* a rear toe piece.

Trick Skis

Manufacturers have now designed trick skis for beginners that are easier to ride and adjust to, and lighter, smoother skies for advanced trickers. Trick skis, as seen in figure 1.4, are shorter and wider than normal skis and have no fins. Again, your ability level is critical in determining which skis are best for you. For beginners, numerous well-designed and well-manufactured fiberglass and foam skis offer the stability and tracking needed to learn how to ride tricks. More experienced trickers prefer carbon or honeycomb skis because of their lighter weight. In either case there are several design factors to consider when selecting trick skis:

Figure 1.4 **A well-designed trick ski.**

- ○ **Rounded top edges.** This feature allows water to slide over the top of the skis during turns.
- ○ **Ski tip area.** On trick skis, the tip area is similar on both the tip and tail to offer better stability. Whether to choose rounded or square depends on your personal preference.
- ○ **Bottom design.** The bottom design should be flat, with or without tracking grooves. These grooves help the skis track but sacrifice rotational speed.
- ○ **Rocker.** On trick skis, the rocker sometimes runs the full length of the ski. However, skis with a short flat spot in the center are ideal because they make surface tricks smoother and edging easier. This rocker pattern makes surface tricks smoother and edging the ski easier.
- ○ **Weight.** Trick skis should be as light as possible for easy turns and good control.
- ○ **Length.** Match the length of your skis with your weight in accordance with table 1.2.

Many trickers are now using different skis for different tricks. For hand tricks, flips, and handle pass tricks, they use bigger and wider trick skis that have

TABLE 1.2 Trick Ski Size Chart

Weight (pounds)	Size (inches)
0-80	36-38
80-120	38-40
120-160	40-42
160-180	42-44
180+	44

Note: Divisions between sizes are approximate. Seek the advice of a coach to assist you in your choice.

hard edges and are more like wakeboards. For toe tricks (tricks done with the rope attached to the foot), skis that have rubber edges and less rocker with a larger flat spot under the foot are best. Hard-shell bindings have become the overwhelming standard for most high-end trickers, but a few are still holdouts for rubber bindings.

Jump Skis

The most dramatic change in jump ski design over the past 10 or so years has been in the length of the skis and the materials they are made of (see figure 1.5). The ability of longer skis to carry speed, hold angle, and create lift has translated into distances once thought impossible. The physical demands of jumping are not to be taken lightly. Designers and manufacturers of jumpers know this and have designed jumpers for every talent level. It is imperative, whether you are a beginner or whether you have jumped over 200 feet, that you get jump skis that are safe and durable and fit your size and skill level. As with trick skis, jumpers are made of carbon, fiberglass, and foam honeycomb and graphite. Regardless of the materials used, several performance characteristics should be considered before buying any set of jumpers:

Figure 1.5 **A jump ski and the equipment you need to jump a long distance safely.**

- **Ski tip.** On jumpers, the ski tip should be wider than the middle of the ski, or at the very least the same width, to create lift.
- **Square edges.** Jump skis have flat, square edges that are more like snow skis on both the top and bottom to promote faster turns and hold angle.
- **Bottom design.** The bottom must be smooth to give full acceleration during cuts.
- **Rocker.** The rocker should be moderate from tip to tail to aid in the tuning and stability of the skis.
- **Flex.** Flex should be softer for beginners and lighter jumpers, and stiffer for more advanced and heavier jumpers.
- **Fins.** The fins should be made of a strong material such as metal, carbon, or plastic.
- **Length.** The ski length should be matched to the weight and skill level of the jumper. The smaller and lighter the skier, the smaller and lighter the jump skis so the skier can control and manage the skis on the water and in the air. Jump skis are sized from 68 to 76 inches for first time jumpers up to jumpers who are cutting at the ramp. Advanced jumpers use jump skis sized at 84 to 92 inches. Size and weight are part of the equation for

finding the right skis for advanced jumpers, but strength, skill, and ability to control the skis should be the major determining factor.

The details of jump skis and jumping equipment are discussed in greater detail in chapter 7.

Bindings for most jumpers are rubber. A few have used hard-shells with great success, but overall they have not caught on the way they have in slalom and trick skiing. Jump binding design may well be the next great performance evolution in the event.

Wakeboards

Wakeboards, such as the one in figure 1.6, are going through a design revolution. Manufacturers are experimenting with new shapes and lighter materials to make the boards easier to edge and turn in the air. Two questions should determine the type of wakeboard that is best for you:

1. What is your riding style?
2. What is your ability level?

Your athletic background (surfing or snow skiing, or snowboarding or skateboarding) can help you decide your riding style. In the past, surfers and skiers often preferred single-tip boards, whereas snowboarders and skateboarders gravitated toward twin-tips. Today, most boarders use twin-tip boards because of the evolution of the tricks being performed and the need to take off and land on both sides and edges of the board.

Similar to slalom skis, an entry-level board needs to track well, be stable, and allow for long cuts outside the wake. A board with a sharp, square rail offers these benefits while keeping the cost down for your first board purchase. The downside to square rails is that they make landings from air tricks more difficult. You have a better chance of catching an edge and taking hard falls with sharp rails. Rounded rails make the landings easier and softer and aren't as likely to catch an edge, making tricks easier.

The lightest boards are made with either honeycomb or carbon graphite and offer significant performance enhancements. There has been some trouble with honeycomb boards breaking, so ask your dealer whether the board you want to buy has had this problem, and if so, whether the manufacturer had remedied the problem.

Figure 1.6 **All geared up for wakeboarding.**

Accessories

For both water skiing and wakeboarding, you will need a few accessories such as a rope, handle, life vest, wetsuit, and gloves. When selecting accessories, *value* is the operative word.

○ **Ropes.** For slalom, the first rope you need to buy is an 80-strand slalom line rather than a 60-strand line. This will give you the most flexibility and durability for the least money. Purchase an eight-loop slalom rope to begin with. The loop lengths for advanced slalom course skiing are shown in detail in chapter 9. They have the added benefit of making it easy to adjust for tricking or boarding and can be used for learning to jump as well. Get a rope made by a reputable manufacturer so you know that the cutoff loops are measured correctly and that the rope is of high quality.

As your skills advance, you will want event-specific ropes. For trick skiing, a poly-e or Spectra line of 12 meters with loops or a few additional rope sections of 1 meter and 1/2 meter will help you set yourself at the proper position behind the boat relative to your riding speed and wake shape desires. For jumping, you want a jump line made from polypropylene or a combination of polypropylene and Spectra depending on the stretch characteristic you prefer. The length is a standard 70 feet 6 1/2 inches (21.5 m). Wakeboarders prefer less stretch, so Spectra or micro fusion ropes are most common in 70-foot (21 m) lengths with loops or sections at 60 feet (18 m) and additional 5-foot (1.5 m) sections.

○ **Handles.** Various types of handles are shown in figure 1.7. If you are simply slalom skiing or jumping, purchase a handle that is easy to grip and hold on to but not so hard that it will tear or rip your hands. A coated bridle is preferred for safety. If you are a big-time boarder, you need a handle that has extra weaving on the rope, which makes body wrap tricks easier and safer. Trickers need a special handle so they can perform toe tricks. The toe-hold harness should be tight, yet comfortable, and have protective wrapping, weaving, and coating on the bridle.

Figure 1.7 **Handles used for slalom skiing, toe tricks, jumping, and wakeboarding.**

○ **Life vests.** Your vest should be a USCG-approved personal flotation device (PFD) with four or five buckles (see figure 1.8). There are nonapproved tournament vests that are lighter and more comfortable, but these should be used only in controlled environments or tournaments. These vests do not count as PFDs when you are checked by the coast guard.

○ **Wetsuits.** The first thing you should determine is what you will be doing in your wetsuit. If you are jumping, spend the money and buy a quality jump suit that will withstand the impact of jumping (refer to figure 1.5). For winter skiing, a full suit or a dry suit is recommended. The best value is a three-quarter suit (see figure 1.9). This suit is warm but still light and more flexible than a full or dry suit. A shorty top is ideal for cooler days or to help keep the morning chill off . The secret is to buy the right suit for your type of skiing.

○ **Gloves, braces, and protective gear.** Gloves are another item you should consider buying before you hit the water. Try on several pairs, and look for features such as double-stitched seams, padded or Kevlar palms, and tight wrist straps that prevent the gloves from sliding up your hand. You may want to consider glove liners or protectors if you plan to spend lots of time on the water. They will keep you skiing longer and having more fun. Back braces, leg protectors, and skiing shorts should be used if you have special needs or problems, or if you feel more comfortable with them. The choice is yours.

○ **Miscellaneous items.** One final consideration is sun protection. A good, full hat and sunscreen are a must, as are quality sunglasses. You may also want to throw in some soap or binding slime to reduce wear and tear on your bindings. You could also carry some type of muscle ache cream just in case.

Figure 1.8 **Proper vests include USCG-approved vests (right) and lighter vests (left) that should be used only for tournaments.**

Figure 1.9 **A three-quarter suit is warm and flexible. A shorty top can also provide warmth.**

Choosing the Best Boat

You can ski behind almost anything: fishing boats, runabouts, skiffs, and even personal watercraft. I grew up skiing behind a 40-horsepower Johnson slapped on the transom of a 14-foot (4.3 m) aluminum flat boat. The minimum power requirement to pull an adult is in the 50- to 100-horsepower range depending on your size, but if you are looking for a great family boat that provides plenty of room, dependability, and ideal skiing, look no further than the inboards on the market today, many of which perform and handle better than the best outboards and stern drives on the market. The inboards of today are no longer just for tournament skiers; they combine the best skiing qualities with roominess for entire families and the ease of maintenance they are famous for. However, a ski boat is an investment in fun, so the most important thing is to get on the water regardless of the power pulling you.

As with any purchase, you'll want the best value for your dollar. Select a boat constructed with high-quality, durable materials, and read the warranties and learn about maintenance. A ski boat should be responsive, have little or no dead rise, and plane off quickly. (Dead rise is the amount the bow lifts when you take off out of the hole.) Once on plane, the boat should be able to hold a constant speed even at lower speeds of 12 to 18 mph (19 to 29 km/h) for tricking, and maintain a straight path even with a skier pulling on the rope. Maintaining speed at a lower speed is a major problem for outboard and stern drives and makes pulling children and lighter skiers or trickers extremely difficult. The driver should not have to fight the wheel to get the boat to track straight, especially in the slalom course. The boat should be able to corner without heeling over on its side and have excellent maneuvering ability at slow speeds.

Wakes can be a major stumbling block for the beginner and for smaller, lighter skiers. The wakes for slalom and jump should be as small as possible with a minimum rooster tail between them. For tricking and boarding at speeds of 12 to 20 mph (19 to 32 km/h), the wakes should be clean and crisp with a sharp rise and flat table behind the boat.

The steering and throttle need to be smooth and easy to control from the driver's seat, with a forearm rest for comfort and drivability. The boat should be fitted with two speedometers and standard running gauges for oil, battery, temperature, and fuel. Additionally, the windshield must not obstruct the drivers view and should be fitted with a rearview mirror. The driver should always be able to see anything in front.

Figure 1.10   **A sturdy tower and pylon make for a solid pull.**

Ideally, a tow pylon is located in the middle of the boat in front of the engine (see figure 1.10). For wakeboarding, a sturdy tower is a must. In outboards and stern drives, this is usually not possible, so a rear pylon is used. This type of pylon allows the skier to move the boat and makes steering difficult. Because of the steering difficulties caused by rear pylons and their proximity to the engine, use caution, and make sure the rope does not get tangled in the prop.

Preparing the Boat Crew

On the pro tour one of the most critical jobs is boat driver, and the same can be said for any weekend outing on the lake. The boat driver is the captain of the ship and therefore responsible for the safety of the skier and the crew. As is the case with any leader, the driver's performance, attitude, and safety consciousness set an example for the crew to follow. In water skiing, as in all sports, safety is a function of taking the time to prevent problems and preparing for them if they do arise. Safety may not seem like the most interesting topic, but it is an important one that no one can ignore. The following driving patterns and tips, as well as rules for observers, can help guarantee everyone's safety.

Driving Tips

As with any learned skill, the only way to become a great boat driver is to spend time behind the wheel and keep your ears and mind open to recommendations to improve your driving. Here are eight tips to improve your driving no matter your ability:

- **Think of the skier.** Each skier deserves the best pull you can give regardless of ability. Pay attention to the skier's size, weight, and skiing style. You can develop a feel of where the skier pulls and adapt your driving likewise.

- **Know the local conditions.** Before you pull the skier, figure out the boat path and pattern that will minimize backwash and boat rollers while giving the skier the longest, straightest setups possible. Once you determine the best pattern, follow it exactly each time. By doing so, you will create smooth water, develop familiarity and consistency, and have less chance of hitting anything in the water.

- **Test the boat before pulling the first skier.** Check the boat for handling characteristics, acceleration, and overall responsiveness before pulling a skier. If the boat is not adequate or if you cannot fix the problems, get another boat or find a driver who can adapt to the boat. Under no circumstances should you let your ego get in the way of taking yourself out of the boat. I once saw world record driver Tommy Harrington throw up his hands in frustration, get out of the boat, and ask another driver to pull the event. This was not just a backyard tournament, either; it was the U.S. Open. Tommy is a truly great driver. By not letting his ego get in the way and allowing another driver who was comfortable with that boat to drive the event, he further proved that he is a skier's driver.

Figure 1.11 **The proper way to hold the throttle.**

○ **Develop proper acceleration and throttle control.** Proper acceleration and throttle control aids both the beginner and the advanced skier. Hold the throttle like an egg. Use your thumb, index, and middle finger to keep a constant, gentle pressure on the throttle as shown in figure 1.11. Use your thumb and wrist to control acceleration and the middle finger to control deceleration. Leverage your arm against the gunnel or armrest, letting the throttle movement come through the fingers and wrist and not the arm. The key is to be smooth and consistent with the throttle.

○ **Grip the wheel properly.** The best position is to grip the steering wheel with the left hand at the 10 or 11 o'clock position. This gives you leverage and control to turn and react to the pull of the skier. A strong skier will most likely pull the boat around a bit. The secret is to anticipate the pull and use smooth, controlled adjustments. Radical, quick, or jerky steering will make things difficult for the skier, so stay calm and try to work with the skier's rhythm.

○ **Keep a straight path.** Picking a spot on the horizon and driving to it will help you prevent oversteering. Your focus should be down course, and your eyes should constantly be scanning the area for other boats or debris that could hamper the skier.

○ **Use the tachometer instead of the speedometer.** Speedometers move as the skier pulls the boat. If you react to the speedometer (which does not respond immediately to actual speeds), you will have large swings in your speed. By maintaining a constant rpm, you will respond to the skier's pull in actual time and not have to move the throttle as much, leading to a more consistent pull. The trick is to learn which rpm reading correlates to a given speed. This is learned through practice and by taking timed passes.

○ **Learn proper driving patterns.** For beginners, a boat pattern that is easy to negotiate is a large loop usually done in a counterclockwise fashion. This pattern does not require the skier to cross the wakes, and the larger turns prevent the whip effect that can occur when a skier gets caught on the outside of the wakes during a turn. If the skier does get caught on the whip, you should cut back the throttle quickly to prevent the skier from hitting shore or taking a bad fall. Once a skier can safely cross the wakes and ski over the boat rollers, a dumbbell pattern is preferred (see figure 1.12). This pattern provides long, straight runs and allows the boat wakes to disperse, leaving the skier with calm water for the next run.

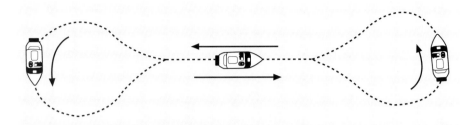

Figure 1.12   **The dumbbell driving pattern.**

When the skier falls, there are several things you must do to ensure the skier's safety and to keep the water calm for the next run. When the skier goes down, pull back on the throttle, turn the steering wheel to the side the skier has fallen on, and idle around the turn before accelerating back to the skier. This prevents boat rollers from ruining the calm water. Slow the boat down well before getting back to the skier, and approach the skier on the driver's side of the boat approximately 15 feet (4.6 m) away from the skier. Always pass the skier downwind or down current to avoid having the wind or current push the boat into the skier, and make sure the boat is in neutral as you pass the skier. There are two methods for picking up a fallen skier: the half-turn method (figure 1.13) and the keyhole method (figure 1.14). Because both are acceptable, choose based on the direction the skier would like to go.

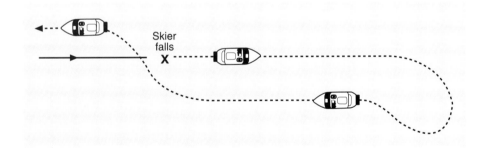

Figure 1.13   **The half-turn method for picking up a skier.**

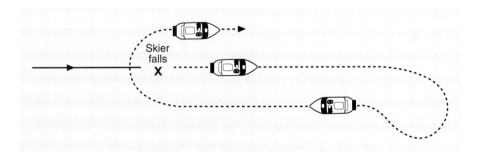

Figure 1.14   **The keyhole method for picking up a skier.**

Observing

The observer is an essential part of any crew. Although some states do not require an observer, I recommend that you never ski without one in the boat. The responsibility of the observer is threefold:

1. Keep the driver informed of the skier's progress.

2. Keep the driver informed of the skier's signals.

3. Assist the driver in being aware of safety hazards.

Selecting a Ski Site

Every skier's dream is to live on a private ski lake with banks perfectly sloped to prevent backwash and tall trees to keep the wind from disturbing the water. Unfortunately, most of us can't afford this utopian luxury and have to make the best of public lakes and rivers. Luckily, numerous public bodies of water fit the description of the perfect lake rather well.

From a safety and skiability standpoint, there are a couple of things to look for when scouting out a ski site. Ideally, an area should be 2,000 to 2,400 feet (610 to 732 m) in length and 250 to 300 feet (76 to 91 m) wide. These dimensions allow for comfortable setups for slalom and jump courses and ample room for trick runs. You should always run the boat at least 100 feet (30.5 m) from the shore so the skier does not ski into the bank. Although it is possible to ski on shorter bodies of water, be cautious because your setups and turns will be tight and you will need to accelerate rapidly.

Now that you're ready with the latest and best gear and a top-quality ski boat, you're ready to hit the water.

Chapter 2

Physical Conditioning

All it takes is a visit to the starting dock of any pro event to realize that long gone are the days when athletes and coaches shunned weightlifting for fear that it might hinder the performance of fine motor skill and disturb correct technique. Today, there is no denying the fact that a high level of strength and conditioning is a prerequisite to superior speed, quickness, power, endurance, and overall performance. In a talk Olympian Jeff Galloway once gave prior to a marathon, he put the need for physical conditioning succinctly: "The single greatest cause of improvement is remaining injury-free to train." This may well be the most compelling reason to increase the strength and endurance component of your training. A well-designed sport-specific strength and conditioning program will improve performance and is the best insurance against injury.

Typically, bodybuilding or Olympic weightlifting–style programs dominate the training regimes of skiers and boarders. Many are surprised to learn that these types of regimes fall well short of what is required to fulfill their potential on the water. Yes, these types of training have their place, but proper training for strength, power, speed, and quickness behind the boat requires a more refined approach than simply lifting heavy weights as many times as possible. Unlike bodybuilding programs, whose only aim is to increase the size and appearance of muscles, a strength training program for on-the-water competition or recreation must develop both explosive power and muscular endurance to meet the demands of the event. Developing power and muscular endurance simultaneously without one negating the other requires careful planning and execution.

The planning and execution of a training regime begin with establishing a baseline measurement of strength. A trainer or your doctor can help you collect data that will help you build the best program for you and assess your improvement along the way. You will need accurate measurements of height, weight, and body fat percentage. You also need to determine your 1-repetition maximum for the bench press and squat and a measure of your muscular endurance.

To determine your 1-repetition maximum, warm up and then lift as much weight as you can for one repetition for each exercise. Use a spotter to prevent injury. To get a measure of muscular endurance, count the number pull-ups and sit-ups you can perform in one minute, and time how long you can hold a back extension. These data will help you determine the areas in which you need to improve and set fitness goals that will lead to on-water success.

Periodization and Seasonal Planning

The most effective approach to strength training for all water sport events is a periodized training plan. This gives you the best chance of peaking physically at the right time and prevents overtraining. An overall training program usually focuses on a one-year period or season, which is subdivided into three segments: preparation (preseason), competition (in-season), and transition (off-season). The key is to coordinate your strength training program with the phases of a typical season so you peak as your competitive season starts and for the most important events during your season. You should divide your sport-specific strength development and conditioning into distinct phases like those of your overall season. The program that follows describes the phases and explains how they work to accommodate performance peaks needed in a typical season.

1. Basic Strength and Cardiorespiratory Fitness

This first phase of strength training and conditioning occurs at the start of the preparation phase. The immense power of boats today as well as the extreme biomechanical forces placed on the body as it is slung from side to side at the end of a rope behind a boat, stresses the rectus abdominis, latissimus dorsi, gluteus maximus, quadriceps, and forearm flexors with a high intensity. It makes good sense to give these muscle groups specific attention when doing basic strength training. Likewise, you need to have endurance and the ability to recover rapidly. You can achieve these goals with cardiorespiratory fitness.

The objective of basic strength training is to prepare your body for more strenuous resistance training later in the season. Targeting all of the major muscle groups, tendons, ligaments, and joints provides a foundation of fitness that will help prevent injury and allow for consistent improvement throughout the season. The amount of time you need to develop a foundation before you move on to more strenuous training depends on your current level of fitness. That said, even very fit athletes need to complete a phase of basic strength training during the year to help correct muscle imbalances that often develop during the competitive part of the season. Frequently, one side of the body becomes stronger than the other side, or the extensor and flexor muscles in one or more parts of the body do not develop evenly. Other muscle groups may be neglected altogether. If these imbalances are not corrected, they can lead to injuries.

Your abdominal muscles and oblique muscles (those located toward the side of your abdomen) represent the core of all strength and are vital to maintaining balance. Weak abdominal muscles and poor fitness are closely associated. Low back pain, poor posture, inflexibility, and breathing problems can all be linked to abdominal weakness. A weakness in your core will predispose you to injury and undermine your attempts to improve on the water. James Loehr, EdD, recommends a minimum of 200 curl-ups or modified sit-ups a day for athletes in training. That may seem excessive, but it emphasizes the importance of strong abdominal muscles in water skiing. Testing performed on pro skiers at the U.S. Olympic Training Center revealed that top water skiers have extremely strong abdominal muscles. Start easy and build up to the recommended 200 reps a day.

The amount of cardiorespiratory stress you should expose yourself to is determined by the event you wish to excel in. Your heart and lungs must be challenged and trained to meet the physical, mental, and emotional energy requirements of your event. Two types of cardio work are needed: aerobic and anaerobic. Both are vital to basic fitness.

Aerobic (meaning "with oxygen") conditioning is the ability to sustain low-intensity exercise for long periods. A technical definition of good aerobic conditioning is the ability to maintain 70 to 85 percent of heart rate reserve (HRR) for 30 to 90 minutes. HRR is the difference between a person's measured or predicted maximum heart rate and his or her resting heart rate. Recent studies recommend exercise that involves both upper- and lower-body movement, such as jogging and cross-country skiing simulation, three to five days a week. Aerobic training is used primarily in the off-season to build a solid fitness foundation before beginning more strenuous on-water training. Aerobic training also has benefits during the ski season; it facilitates rapid muscular recovery during competition.

Anaerobic (meaning "without oxygen") conditioning, also known as interval training, is performed by doing higher-intensity exercise for shorter periods. Technically, anaerobic exercise requires that you maintain 85 to 95 percent of your heart rate reserve for one to three minutes followed by a short rest and another period of exercise. The goal of interval training is to stress the anaerobic system to its maximum limit in a repetitive cycle with a fixed work-to-rest ratio. As a result of the repetition, the aerobic system gets a good workout as well. The work-to-rest ratio should be 90 seconds of work to 30 seconds of rest. The HRR should be 85 to 95 percent during the work stages and 70 to 75 percent during rest periods. Examples of interval training are four 400-meter runs (90 seconds) or four 800-meter bike sprints, with a slow jog or bike pace (30 seconds) equal to 75 percent HRR between sprints two to four times a week. These sessions should be performed during the preseason and into the competitive season, during which the intensity peaks.

The largest portion of cardiorespiratory training should consist of activities that are specific to anaerobic conditioning, such as interval training. Cross-country skiing, stair climbing, in-line skating, rowing, cycling, and running are all excellent activities for improving cardiorespiratory conditioning. The secret is to perform them at the recommended volumes and intensities. High-intensity interval training requires that you have a general fitness level that will tolerate the stress placed on your body. You can develop this general fitness by improving your aerobic conditioning.

2. Maximum Strength

Maximum strength training is the next phase of strength training and conditioning. Depending on your event, the amount of time spent on maxing out strength will vary. Strength and power athletes spend more time in this phase than endurance athletes, for example. The goal of maximum strength training is not necessarily to increase the size of a muscle (hypertrophy). The goal of strength training is to build neuromuscular adaptations that are favorable to most sports. Water skiers and wakeboarders benefit most from increasing their lean body mass by adding muscular strength.

Two principles will help you develop your maximum strength: overload and specificity. These principles apply to all types of strength training but are particularly important to the maximum strength phase.

The overload principle says that to increase the physical capacity of your muscles, you must progressively exercise at a level above what your muscles are accustomed to. The three variables of the overload principle are frequency, intensity, and time (FIT). *Frequency* refers to the number of days an exercise is performed per week. *Intensity* refers to the workload at which the exercise is performed. *Time* refers to the amount of time spent performing the exercise.

All three overload variables must be included in a training program to make the program successful. The overload principle applies to on- and off-the-water training, and the variables must be balanced carefully to avoid overtraining.

The principle of specificity refers to the adaptation that takes place as a result of training. Muscle development is specific to the type of stress placed on the muscles. The objective of resistance training is to increase the strength of muscles and other soft tissues (ligaments, tendons) to improve performance and prevent injury. Resistance training programs should emphasize strengthening muscles that are specific to skiing and boarding and progressively overload these muscles.

In other words, athletes need to train movements rather than muscles. For example, a jump skier needs to train using a movement that is similar to the movement he would use to jump off the ramp. The muscles involved in ski jumping include calves, quadriceps, hamstrings, and gluteus maximus. You could train these muscles separately with exercises such as the heel raise, leg extension, and leg curl. A better choice, though, would be the barbell squat because the movement pattern of this exercise is similar to that of the jump off the ramp. The squat jump would be even more specific to ski jumping, and would provide the best results for a jumper's performance.

3. Conversion

The conversion of maximum strength to sport-specific power occurs late in the preparation phase and continues into the competitive phase. To improve performance, you must convert your maximum strength into sport-specific power, muscular endurance, or both. This results in explosive power, which you have no doubt witnessed in some athletes. Just as athletes can be extremely muscular and lack the strength to perform certain movements, so can some be exceptionally strong but lack significant power. Most athletic movements occur much more rapidly and demand significantly more power than lifting maximum loads. If maximum strength is not converted into sport-specific power, athletic performance will not improve—certainly not to the extent that it could.

The conversion of maximum strength to sport-specific power is accomplished by overloading the muscles while performing the specific movement in various ways or for progressively longer periods. Water skiing is an anaerobic activity because you typically have about 5 minutes of all-out activity that raises the heart rate to high levels. Although the brief rest period between slalom, trick, or wakeboard passes or jumps does allow for recovery, testing has shown that the heart rate rises when the skier leaves the dock and does not decrease significantly until the run is over. Therefore, skiing without rest periods or skiing at slower speeds can convert strength to power by focusing on the muscles most needed in the movement.

Plyometric exercises are another way of converting strength to power. Biomechanical analysis of all forms of water skiing has shown that rapid and powerful movements in response to the forces imposed on the skier by the boat, rope, wake, and skis can be improved with plyometrics. Plyometrics improve speed, quickness, reaction time, and jumping ability. The primary objective is to increase the excitability of the nervous system for improved reactive ability of the neuromuscular system. Improving the functioning of the neuromuscular system produces quicker and more explosive movements.

Exercise caution when performing plyometric exercises. When they are performed correctly, the results can be incredible; however, when overused or used incorrectly, plyometrics can ruin your season or career as a result of the extreme stress placed on the body. Before beginning plyometrics, develop a strength base. The following plyometric exercises can help improve your performance.

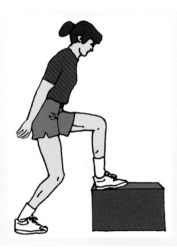

STEP-UP

Start with a step 6 to 12 inches (15 to 30 cm) high.

1. Step onto the step planting the entire foot on it.
2. Bring both feet onto the step; then step off one leg at a time.
3. Repeat with the other foot.

Start with a 30-second exercise time and increase as you adapt to the exercise.

SIDE JUMP

Set up a barrier that you can jump over sideways. You can use small cones or a rope. It's best to start with a barrier that is about 3 inches (7.6 cm) high.

1. Jump from one side of the barrier to the other.
2. As soon as your feet land on the other side, explode into the next jump.

Increase your speed and time as you improve.

BOUNDING

This exercise can be done on either one or two legs.

1. Push off and jump as high and as far as you can.
2. Upon landing, jump explosively up and forward with a strong arm swing.

To increase the challenge, you can set out a series of blocks or obstacles along your path to jump over. Increase your yardage and time as you adapt to the exercise.

LUNGE

Stand with both feet together.

1. Step forward with one leg until the knee of that leg bends to a 90-degree angle. The lower leg should be perpendicular to the floor. Keep the opposite leg straight.
2. Push off explosively, and return the forward leg to the starting position.
3. Repeat with the opposite leg.

4. Maintenance

You've probably heard the saying "use it or lose it," which is based on a principle of conditioning known as reversibility. This principle refers to the fact that gains are lost when overload is not continued. In fact, fitness is lost twice as fast as it is gained. It is important to incorporate resistance training and aerobic conditioning into your in-season training program to maintain the fitness level gained in the off-season. Research has shown that strength and conditioning gains can be maintained with minimal training (as seldom as once a week) as long as the intensity of training is sufficient to incite overload.

5. Active Recovery

At the end of every season, you may have some minor bumps, bruises, pulls, and strains that may not have had the chance to heal fully. This is when you need the active recovery phase. A mental and physical break from structured training and the grind of competition is crucial for every athlete. The active recovery phase consists of a complete break from all types of strength training for several weeks. If your break is longer than 3 to 4 weeks, however, your fitness level, particularly your level of strength and power, can become the victim of reversibility.

During this period of rest you should maintain an active stretching routine to stay flexible and help your body recover from any injuries that linger from season. The purpose of stretching is to increase flexibility, relieve muscle soreness, prevent injury, warm up and cool down muscles, provide greater potential for athletic skills, and aid in recovery from injury. Active isolated stretching (AIS), developed by kinesiologist Aaron L. Mattes, has shown unprecedented success in improving the range of motion and reducing and preventing injuries.

AIS entails holding each stretch position for one to two seconds and then returning to the starting position and resting the muscles for two seconds. Then, you ease into the stretch again. The two-second limitation is what distinguishes AIS from traditional stretching. You can augment AIS in two ways. One is to contract the muscle group opposing the muscle you are stretching to help move the muscle to be stretched into a position that provides a greater stretch. The second option is to enhance the stretch by using a rope or your hands to gently move the muscle to a position that provides a greater stretch. As with all stretching, you should never force your muscles beyond a feeling of minor irritation. Stretching should not be painful.

AIS is great, but you must find what works best for you and keep working on improving your flexibility. Try incorporating the stretches that follow into your training routine and warm-up. According to Aaron L. Mattes, these stretches are most likely to help water skiers and wakeboarders increase flexibility and prevent injuries.

NECK LATERAL FLEXION

Perform this stretch on both sides of your neck for 8 to 10 repetitions.

1. While standing straight, press your ear to your shoulder by contracting cervical flexors.
2. You can assist with your hand by gently pulling down on your head.

NECK ROTATION

Do 8 to 10 stretches and repeat on the opposite side.

1. Rotate your chin to your shoulder.
2. Assist with your hand by pressing lightly on your jaw.

HORIZONTAL SHOULDER FLEXION

This stretches the external shoulder rotators. Do this stretch for both arms for 8 to 10 repetitions.

1. Place your arm across your chest.
2. Reach the opposite arm around midway between the shoulders and pectoral (chest) muscles.
3. Use the opposite hand on the elbow to assist the stretch across the body at the end of the movement.

HORIZONTAL ABDUCTION

To stretch the pectoral (chest) muscles, complete 6 to 8 repetitions on each side.

1. Place your wrist against a post or wall with your palm forward and at shoulder height.
2. Rotate or move forward away from the support until you feel a stretch.

SINGLE-LEG PELVIC TILT

This stretch is for the low back and gluteus maximus. Perform 10 or more repetitions.

1. Lie on your back. Flex the exercising knee and pull it forward toward your chest by contracting your hip flexor and abdominal muscles.
2. Place your hands behind your thigh to provide assistance at the end of the free movement.

HAMSTRING STRETCH

The hamstring muscle is stretched by a constant contraction of the quadriceps. Complete two sets of 10, alternating legs after each set.

1. Lie on your back. Wrap a band or towel around one foot and hold the ends with your hands. Lift the leg slowly with your quadriceps. Do not allow the leg to bend at any point in the movement.
2. Give gentle assistance with a rope or your hands at the end of the movement.

QUADRICEPS STRETCH

This stretch is for the lower hip and quads. Two sets of 10 with alternating legs are recommended.

1. Lie on your side. Bend your bottom knee and place your hand under the foot to stabilize the leg.
2. Flex the top leg and grab the foot. Contract the abdominal muscles to prevent any forward tilt of the pelvis. Maintain your upper leg in a flexed position throughout the stretch.
3. Contract your gluteus maximus and hamstrings, reaching backward with your hand to give gentle assistance.

TRUNK FLEXION

Perform 10 to 15 repetitions.

1. Begin from an upright sitting position with your legs extended out in front, spread about shoulder-width apart. Maintain a bend in your knees.
2. Exhale, tuck your chin, flex your knees 2 to 3 inches (5 to 7.6 cm), and contract your abdominal muscles strongly as your body curls forward. Avoid any bouncing or rapid movement at the end of the stretch.
3. Use your hands to pull yourself forward at the end of the stretch to get a little more stretch.

TRUNK ROTATION

This stretch is for the thoracic muscles and lumbar rotators. Do 8 to 10 repetitions.

1. Sit with one leg straight. Flex the opposite knee 90 degrees and cross over and rest your foot on the outside of the straight leg.
2. Place the opposite side elbow on the outside of your flexed knee. Place the opposite hand on the ground behind your back for stability.
3. Turn your head and trunk as far as possible away from your midline and assist with elbow pressure against your knee.

ACHILLES TENDON AND CALF STRETCH

Do 8 to 10 repetitions on each foot.

1. Sit with one leg straight. Bring your knee into your chest and grab your foot below the toes.
2. Stretch your calf and Achilles tendon by flexing the ankle and foot dorsal flexor muscles toward your knee.

Sample Strength and Conditioning Training Programs

The strength and conditioning training programs outlined in this section consist of relatively few exercises. This is deliberate, taking into account other training you are expected to complete on the water. To get the most from your training and accommodate any time constraints, make good choices about how to divide your time and energy among the various types of training you need to do. Choosing to work on only the most sport-specific muscles or your weakest muscles will keep the volume of your resistance exercises to a minimum, which will save you time and energy for training behind the boat.

When engaging in training programs, a proper warm-up is essential, and a cool-down is even more important. The purpose of a warm-up is to help the body make the transition from rest to exercise. The objective is to increase the blood flow to the working skeletal muscles and raise the tissue temperature. Your warm-up should include 5 to 10 minutes of light aerobic activity (such as biking or jogging) followed by a stretching, or flexibility, routine. Research has shown that a properly conducted warm-up can reduce the risk of injuries.

The cool-down is extremely important. The cool-down consists of light exercise following a training session. The objective is to gradually return all metabolic functions to preexercise levels. The cool-down also reduces soreness by speeding the removal of lactic acid and other cellular waste from the muscles. Good cool-downs include a light swim if you are at the lake, some stretching, or a slow jog or bike ride. The cool-down should last for 5 to 10 minutes.

All of the recommended strength training programs are organized to work each major muscle group with one or two exercises. Consult a trainer to learn more about these exercises and to help you customize your program. Books such as Jim Stoppani's *Encyclopedia of Muscle & Strength* (2006) can also help you learn how to do these exercises properly. The following tips will help you get the most benefit from the programs outlined in this chapter:

- Use common sense. Your schedule should fit your needs. Consider work, school, and other activities. Listen to your body, and get rest.
- Alter the program to suit your strengths and weaknesses.
- Always include a 10- to 15-minute warm-up and cool-down.
- Always stretch during your warm-up and cool-down.
- Do your cardio workout after your strength workout.
- Never increase the weight or time by more than 5 percent.
- Work large muscles first.
- Accentuate the lowering portion of each repetition.
- Do not sacrifice form in an attempt to lift more weight.
- Include a good nutrition program along with your strength and cardiorespiratory training.

Weekend Warrior Strength and Conditioning Program

If you are a weekend skier or boarder and want to get in shape to have more fun on the water, this is the program for you. This is a great general fitness program that will help you in everything you do. To gauge the amount of weight to lift, use this general rule: If you can do 15 repetitions of a weight, add additional weight; if you can't do 10 repetitions of a weight, reduce the weight.

Exercise or activity	Sets and reps (or duration)
Monday, Wednesday, and Friday	
Sit-up	3 × max reps
Plyometric training:	
Jump rope	2-5 minutes
Step-up	1 minute
Side jump	1 minute
Tuesday	
Squat or leg press	2 × 10-15
Leg curl	10-15
Leg extension	10-15 reps
Aerobic training	20-40 minutes
Thursday	
Bench press	1 × 10-15
Military press	1 × 10-15
Lat pull-down	1 × 10-15
Arm curl	1 × 10-15
Triceps extension	1 × 10-15
Back extension	1 × 10-15
Aerobic training	20-40 minutes

Competition Strength and Conditioning Program

This program is designed for the skier or boarder who wants to compete on an amateur or professional level. The program is based on data accumulated by testing top pro skiers at the U.S. Olympic Training Center. This program develops incredible total body fitness, but does not take your skiing or boarding schedule and other demands into consideration. You must use your own judgment to refine the program to fit your needs and address your weaknesses. You will notice that no activity is listed for the time periods of February 16 through 21 and April 8 through 14. This is intentional. These are periods of time in which you should be resting and doing active recovery with light stretching.

(continued)

Competition Strength and Conditioning Program *(continued)*

Preparation Period
(January 1 to February 15)

This training period lasts for six weeks. The strength training done during this period should be performed at 80 percent of your 1-repetition maximum. Aerobic training is performed at 75 percent HRR, and anaerobic training is performed at 85 percent HRR. During this period, you will rest on Thursdays, Saturdays, and Sundays.

Exercise	Sets and reps (or duration)
Monday and Friday	
Sit-up	3 × max
Squat or leg press	3-5 × 10-15 (weeks 1 and 2) 3-5 × 10-15 (weeks 3 and 4) 1 × max (weeks 5 and 6)
Leg curl	2 × 10-15 (weeks 1 and 2) 2 × 10-15 (weeks 3 and 4) 1 × max (weeks 5 and 6)
Squat or leg press	2 × 10-15
Leg curl	2 × 10-15
Leg extension	2 × 10-15
Bench press	2 × 10-15
Military press	2 × 10-15
Lat pull-down	2 × 10-15
Arm curl	2 × 10-15
Triceps extension	2 × 10-15
Back extension	2 × 10-15
Leg extension	2 × 10-15
Bench press	2 × 10-15
Military press	2 × 10-15
Lat pull-down	2 × 10-15
Arm curl	2 × 10-15
Triceps extension	2 × 10-15
Back extension	2 × 10-15
Aerobic training (Monday only)	30 minutes
Interval training (Friday only)	3-6 intervals

Exercise	Sets and reps (or duration)
Tuesday	
Interval training	4-7 intervals
Plyometric training:	
Jump rope	5-10 minutes
Step-up	2-4 minutes
Side jump	2-4 minutes
Wednesday	
Circuit training:	
Perform 1 minute of aerobic exercise immediately after each of the following strength training exercises.	
Squat or leg press	1 × 10-15 (weeks 1 and 2) 1 × 10-15 (weeks 3 and 4) 1 × 8-10 (weeks 5 and 6)
Leg curl	1 × 10-15
Leg extension	1 × 10-15
Bench press	1 × 10-15
Military press	1 × 10-15
Lat pull-down	1 × 10-15
Arm curl	1 × 10-15
Triceps extension	1 × 10-15
Back extension	1 × 10-15
Plyometric training:	
Jump rope	5-10 minutes
Bounding	2-4 minutes
Side jump	2-4 minutes

Precompetitive Period
(February 22 to April 7)

The precompetitive period also lasts for six weeks. During this period, strength training is performed at 65 percent of your 1-repetition maximum. Aerobic training is performed at 70 percent HRR. Anaerobic training is performed at 90 percent HRR. You should rest on Wednesdays, Saturdays, and Sundays.

Exercise	Sets and reps (or duration)
Monday and Thursday	
Circuit training: Perform 1 minute of aerobic exercise immediately after each of the following strength training exercises.	
Squat or leg press	2 × 10-15
Leg curl	1 × 10-15
Leg extension	1 × 10-15
Bench press	1 × 10-15
Military press	1 × 10-15
Lat pull-down	1 × 10-15
Arm curl	1 × 10-15
Triceps extension	1 × 10-15
Back extension	1 × 10-15
Sit-up	4 × max
Tuesday and Friday	
Interval training	6-10 intervals
Plyometric training: Jump rope	5-10 minutes
Step-up	2-4 minutes
Side jump	2-4 minutes
Lunge	2-4 minutes
Bounding	2-4 minutes

Competitive Period
(April 15 until the season ends)

Strength training is performed at 75 percent of your 1-repetition maximum. Aerobic training is performed at 75 percent HRR. Anaerobic training is performed at 90 percent HRR. On Saturdays and Sundays, you'll be competing. On Monday, you should ski or board only. On Tuesday and Thursday, you should do strength training and on-water training. On Friday, you should rest.

Exercise	Sets and reps (or duration)
Tuesday and Thursday	
Sit-up	3 × max
Squat or leg press	2 × 10-15
Bench press	1 × 10-15
Military press	1 × 10-15
Arm curl	1 × 10-15
Triceps extension	1 × 10-15
Back extension	1 × 10-15
Interval training	5-10 intervals

(continued)

Competition Strength and Conditioning Program *(continued)*

Active Rest Period
(November 1 to December 31)

Strength training is performed at 60 percent of your 1-repetition maximum. Aerobic training is performed at 70 percent HRR. You should rest on Saturdays and Sundays.

Exercise	Sets and reps (or duration)
Monday and Thursday	
Sit-up	3 × max
Squat or leg press	3-5 × 15-20 (weeks 1 and 2)
	3-5 × 15-20 (weeks 3 and 4)
	1 × max (weeks 5 and 6)
Leg curl	2 × 15-20 (weeks 1 and 2)
	2 × 15-20 (weeks 3 and 4)
	1 × max (weeks 5 and 6)
Squat or leg press	2 × 15-20
Leg curl	2 × 15-20
Leg extension	2 × 15-20
Bench press	2 × 15-20
Military press	2 × 15-20
Lat pull-down	2 × 15-20
Arm curl	2 × 15-20
Triceps extension	2 × 15-20
Back extension	2 × 15-20
Leg extension	2 × 15-20
Bench press	2 × 15-20
Military press	2 × 15-20
Lat pull-down	2 × 15-20
Arm curl	2 × 15-20
Triceps extension	2 × 15-20
Back extension	2 × 15-20
Tuesday, Wednesday, and Friday	
Aerobic training	25 minutes (weeks 1 and 2)
	30 minutes (weeks 3 and 4)
	40 minutes (weeks 5 and 6)

Water Skiing Nutrition

Water skiing and wakeboarding require endurance—you spend long hours in the boat or on the lake in the energy-draining sun. However, this is not the type of endurance needed for running a marathon or cross-country skiing. Because water skiing and wakeboarding are vastly different from these types of endurance sports, the nutritional requirements for skiers and boarders are considerably different. Water skiing and wake boarding require bursts of discontinuous explosive energy, with intermittent periods of reduced physical demand or rest. In slalom you drop at the end of the course after a completed pass, in jump you have time between jumps when riding down the lake, in tricking you have setup time between passes or the intentional fall at the end of a trick pass to catch your breath. Robert Hass, MD, author of *Eat to Win,* recommends a balanced diet with the right mixture of protein, fat, and carbohydrate to replenish torn-down muscles and train muscles to use blood sugar and fat efficiently to give you the explosive power you need.

Three food categories—carbohydrate, protein, and fat— supply the fuel for peak performance. Eat these foods in the suggested quantities to meet the nutritional requirements of water skiing and wakeboarding.

Carbohydrate
(50 to 75 percent of total caloric intake)

Cereals

Fresh fruit

Dried fruit

Fruit juice

Potatoes

Brown rice

Pasta

Vegetables (raw or steamed)

Whole-grain breads or pancakes

Protein
(15 to 35 percent of total caloric intake)

Skim milk

Low-fat cheese

Grated parmesan or Romano cheese

Low-fat cottage cheese

Low-fat yogurt

Meat: poultry, fish, shellfish, lean beef, duck, pork, lamb, venison

Legumes: beans, peas, lentils, nuts, seeds

Fat
(5 to 20 percent of total caloric intake)

Olive oil

Vegetable oil (corn, sesame, safflower)

Margarine

Mayonnaise

(Avoid peanut oil, butter, and lard.)

Other Food Items
The following items will help you improve the taste of the foods you eat and are OK in limited quantities:

Butter buds or other low-fat, low-cholesterol butter substitute.

Oil-free salad dressings

Vinegar

Condiments (mustard, ketchup, steak sauce, barbecue sauce)

Lemon or lime juice

Bacon bits or soy bits

Sugar- and salt-free spices

Beverages
Water is the preferred beverage, but other options are OK in limited quantities.

Water

Coffee

Vegetable juices

Hot chocolate (reduced-calorie versions)

Diet soda (without caffeine)

Another area of nutrition that athletes often wonder about is nutritional supplements. Although nutritional supplements are not a necessity, such supplements have evolved considerably over the past few years. Current research has demonstrated that a multivitamin is better than trying to piece together a mix of vitamins and other supplements. Multivitamins are also more convenient because they eliminate the measuring, counting, and weighing of foods. Meal replacements or supplements that are scientifically engineered to balance vitamins, minerals, carbohydrate, protein, and trace elements that the body needs can help speed recovery and promote strength gains.

Chapter 3

Fundamental Movements and Boat Motion

When you watch an Olympic gymnast fluently dancing, spinning, and flipping on a 4-inch balance beam or a snow skier smoothly blast down the mountain, you might be struck by how effortless the movements look. You might even fantasize that you could do that. All it takes is standing on a balance beam and trying to muster up the courage to even take a shot at doing a back flip to cure you of that wild idea. Making it look easy, that efficiency of movement, is one of the true signs that the athlete has mastered the sport or a particular move. Flow of movement, confidence, power, sensitivity, and precision are all conveyed by the best of the best in any endeavor. These qualities stem from another common characteristic of great athletes—a detailed understanding of their bodies in space and the movements needed for moving in a coordinated effort while managing the internal and external forces exerted on them.

Water skiing and wakeboarding require the application of extreme forces and torques in many directions. These sports require exquisite timing and a lot of strength, and consume large amounts of physical energy. Understanding these sports on this level involves an understanding of physics. In general terms sport biomechanics and sport engineering are applied physics. Modern biomechanics is the study of the forces underlying motion, or kinetics, and how to measure them. Force, technique, speed, coordination, and timing are well within the area of biomechanics.

If you ask top skier Jamie Beauchesne about slalom, or Freddy Krueger about jumping, or coach Mike Ferraro about wakeboarding or tricking, you will likely get an education on intricate positions, movements, and managing and controlling the transfer of power from the boat to the ski or board. They will talk about two things: motion (the force of the boat being transferred through the rope to the body) and movement (the way to position the body to transfer the motion of the boat to the skis or board). The goal is to get the board or skis where they need to be to efficiently use the motion of the boat. These two things create the kinetic chain of these sports, and understanding that chain is an essential part of achieving proper technique and body position for every event.

Boat and Rope Motion

One of the great innovations in water skiing and wakeboarding has been speed control systems, which allow the boat to respond to the forces that are transmitted to it via the rope. As the skier or wakeboarder, you must work with and adjust your style and movement to be in sync with the pull of the boat. Additionally, because the rope stretches, you need to know when and how to use the rope stretch to your advantage.

Speed Control Systems

Speed control systems have resulted in a drastic improvement in towed-boat sports, making at least part of the driver's job much easier and more predictable. These improvements have mostly occurred with the throttle or the force and timing of the boat's acceleration. The speed control systems respond to the skier or boarder's movements. The more predictable and consistent the motion of the boat is, the better the athlete can develop movements and timing to work with the boat's pattern of acceleration (programmed by the speed control system).

The current state of the art in speed control systems used in competition is the Zero Off GPS-based system. The driver accelerates the boat as normal, but at the set speed for each event, the system takes over accelerations and decelerations, maintaining the speed to the 1/1,000 of a second. Understanding when the boat will accelerate or decelerate is essential in developing your movement style and equipment setup. After multiple iterations, designs, and versions created with the help of Andy Mapple, Freddy Krueger, and other top skiers and riders, the current version of Zero Off uses the letters A, B, and C to differentiate a skier or boarder's preference for when the boat increases rpm in response to the skier or boarder's movements, thus accelerating. A selection on A has the most delay, and C has the least delay. This means that at the moment of load, when the skier stretches the rope and slows the boat down, C accelerates the quickest, whereas A will have the largest delay before the boat accelerates.

The Zero Off system also uses the numbers 1, 2, and 3 to indicate the intensity and duration of the rpm increase. The number 1 has the smallest rpm increase, but for the longest duration (long and soft). The number 3 has the largest rpm increase, but for a short duration (short and hard). The numbers 1, 2, and 3 also describe the threshold of when the system reacts to the skier. When you load the rope, you must load it enough to break the necessary preset threshold, causing the system to engage. Setting 1 has a lower preset threshold and so requires less skier load on the rope before the system engages. Setting 3, on the other hand, has a higher preset threshold and requires a higher skier load to activate the system.

The letters and numbers combine to offer a variety of speed control settings (see figure 3.1). Understanding these settings can be difficult. A theory created by competitive slalom skier Dave Satterfield, helps explain how the Zero Off system works. Satterfield explains that at the extremes, you have the following settings:

- A1 has a delay after you start pulling. It has a long, soft pull.
- A3 has a delay after you start pulling. It has a short, hard pull.
- C1 starts pulling right after you do. It has a long, soft pull.
- C3 starts pulling right after you do. It has a short, hard pull.

You may need some help determining how to find the best Zero Off setting for you. Consider specifically your balance when you tip or roll your ski or board on edge and load, or stretch, the rope. If the rope feels soft or mushy and you are losing balance away from the boat and then being pulled toward the boat, you need a higher setting (more toward C and 3). If you are getting stuck in a lean or cannot control your position across the course, go to a higher setting. Larger skiers and aggressive skiers often have trouble finding their balance with the timing of the system. Additionally, you need to assess your balance when you want to advance or break free from the boat. If you feel like the rope is getting pulled away from you after the wakes, then move toward the C settings. Conversely, if you are having difficulty establishing and maintaining your edge or tip of the ski or board or are being pulled up or toward the boat, move your setting down toward the A and 1 settings.

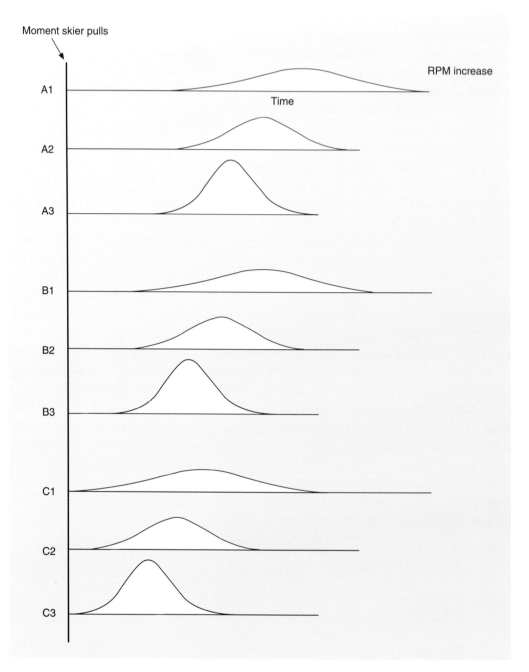

Figure 3.1   Response time and RPM increases for various speed control systems settings.
Reprinted with permission of Dave Satterfield.

Rope Stretch

A few years back I worked with a PhD physicist at the University of Alabama, Birmingham, to develop an off-water water skiing simulation system. As we discussed each event and the movements of the skier and motion of the boat, the factor that he said was most difficult to simulate and vital to creating an accurate model was the rope stretch. He took it one step further and said that rope stretch and knowing how to manage and control it is the most important element of the sport. Going even further, he said that the ski jumper who can time the recoil of the rope stretch most efficiently and at the correct time will achieve a significantly greater distance than the jumper who has the rope recoil either too early or too late.

Although these were just observations without research to back them up, they made me want to learn more about the stretch of the rope in relation to the movement of the boat, my balance, and my position on the water and in the course. To feel how rope stretch, both too much and not enough, can affect your balance, timing, and ability to transfer motion into movement, try to take a slalom pass with a Kevlar rope or wakeboard with a jump line. The lack of stretch in a Kevlar slalom line makes the pull from the boat hit you so hard that it pulls you off the edge of the ski, making it impossible to maintain direction across the wakes. A spongy or stretch rope creates so much delay in the pull from the boat that you lose balance when you pull on the rope.

Fundamental Movements

When the power of the boat hits your hand, you must get your body in the correct position to effectively and efficiently transfer that power of motion to your skis or board. The board or skis are set up and designed to do certain things and react in particular ways in response to your movements or positions at particular speeds. Most important is getting the skis or board into the position that gives you strength, balance, and control.

Skiers and boarders develop a style based on body type and strength, previously developed sport skills, and life experiences, as well as coaching. Their movements involve both gross body adjustments of the head, chest, back, and legs and imperceptible adjustments of the eyes and toes. Proper movements align the body for maximum strength, balance, and coordination, providing efficient use of the boat's motion to move the skis or board to the correct position. Inefficient movements cause breakdowns in the kinetic chain of transferring the boat's motion through the body to the skis or board.

A breakdown in movement is your weakest link and leads to mistakes on the water. This is the first area you should train to improve. A great diagnostic tool for determining where your movements fall apart or break down is to review what happens to you at the end of a long practice set. This is typically when your weakest movements take over. Think about what happens after doing 15 well-executed correct reps of the bench presses and what happens after 20 or 25 reps. In any athletic endeavor, the weakest muscle group tires first. On the water, this causes a chain reaction that affects your edge control, balance, pressure control, and rotation.

Proper biomechanical movements can be learned, changed, and developed. A solution may be as simple as a slight adjustment in equipment—say, changing your speed control setting or binding placement to allow you to tip properly for edge control resulting in better balance. In rare cases a solution may involve a highly sophisticated and complex rebuilding of your style. In most cases, though, the purpose of the adjustment is to maintain an aligned, balanced, and strong position that allows you to manage the rope and boat motion. With this position dialed in, you will be able to perform a variety of movement combinations with accuracy, finesse, timing, and power.

Tipping to Create Edge Control

Tipping the skis or board affects the way the edges contact the water's surface and is the building block for all skiing and boarding. Tipping movements establish ski or board angle and direction change as well as directly affect the control of your water speed, your balance, and your response or adaption to the water conditions and boat motion. Tipping is critical because it creates the dynamic interaction between the water's surface and the body.

Tipping is done with the foot, ankle, and leg and is the first movement to activate the kinetic chain encouraging the rest of the body to maintain balance. Because these movements occur closest to the water, they establish the base of support and body alignment to harness the power of the boat. The two types of tipping are heel-side and toe-side tipping (see figure 3.2) on a wakeboard or, to a lesser degree, on a trick ski and medial and lateral tipping (see figure 3.3) done with the arches and outside of the foot. When done properly, tipping results in a smooth, continuous movement with controlled speed, angle, and balance. When you are struggling with tipping, it takes effort to get the edges of the ski or board to grip the water. Turns are an effort, and the harder you push, the more your balance and control get out of kilter.

Figure 3.2 Tipping on the *(a)* heel side and *(b)* toe side help wakeboarders and trick skiers maintain balance.

Figure 3.3 *(a)* Medial and *(b)* lateral tipping on jump skis.

Two methods are used to align, or stack, the body to maintain tipping and establish edge control: inclination and angulation. Most slalom skiers use inclination, as shown in figure 3.4. This very strong, powerful position sets an edge and maintains tipping angle. Most trickers and jumpers use angulations, as shown in figure 3.5, which means that the skier creates angles between body segments. The upper body remains vertical while the hips, knees, and ankles create angles and set the edge.

Figure 3.4 **Body position for edge control through inclination.**

Figure 3.5 **Body position for edge control through angulations.**

For efficient tipping and edge control movements, concentrate on keeping your hips and shoulders in alignment with the skis or board during the edge change or tip. Adjustments in tipping for edge control are made with the feet, hips, knees, and ankles while the ski or board is progressively tipped onto its edge. The other movements (pressure adjustments by flexing and extending the legs counterbalancing, and fore–aft balancing) follow tipping movement in achieving the desired turn shape and angle into the wakes.

Flexing and Extending to Set Pressure Control

Pressure control works very closely with tipping for edge control to maintain angle and direction as the boat pulls you down course. How, when, and where you bend and straighten your legs determines the way you link and coordinate changes in direction. The ankles, knees, and hips regulate and adjust to the tipping pressure the skis or board exert as they move through the water. The feeling is like the water is pushing back against the skis or board driving them back into your body. The cause is the pressure of the skis or board against the water created by shorter and sharper changes in direction, thus requiring flexing. Flexing properly done and with good timing results in a floating feeling or a release from the boat that allows you to carry speed as you change direction and set a new tip or edge with an extension of the legs.

For precise flexing and extending for pressure control, work on keeping the tip or shift to the inside edge as smooth and progressively as possible so as not to stop the speed or movement of the skis or board as the turn develops. You will use a more aggressive weight transfer to the inside edge as you advance to upper-level skiing, resulting in more flexing and extending (see figure 3.6). As the angle increases, greater pressure control is needed to control the side-to-side speed of the skier or boarder. Flexion complements other actions in controlling the shape of the turn.

Figure 3.6 **The knees must flex and extend to control the timing and shape of a turn.**

Balancing With Counter and Fore-and-Aft Movements

Brent Larsen, coach and father of the world record–setting trickers Britt and Tawn, emphatically believes that water skiing should be defined as balance in motion. Balance is the skill required to keep the body in equilibrium when it is acted on by external forces; it directly affects our ability to perform other movements properly. Balance addresses how the body's central mass moves in dynamic relation to more specialized peripheral movements of the extremities—the hands, arms, legs, ankles, head, fingers, and toes. Other forces that affect balance may be the result of deliberate actions on the skier's or boarder's part (tipping, counteracting), or a reaction to disturbances (change in boat motion, rope stretch, ski setup, and wind and water conditions).

The two types of balancing movements are counterbalancing and fore–aft balancing. Both of these are initiated by, and interact with, tipping the skis or board as well as how the entire foot is positioned in relation to the surface. The need to sense the sometimes very subtle changes in position is why good foot beds and good foot contact with the ski or board are so critical. Either a forward or backward weight shift (weight on your toes or heels) or side-to-side movement (weight on the inside or outside of your foot) changes your balance point in relation to your upper body. Feeling and working the entire foot and positioning your upper body in relation to those movements are balancing movements.

Counterbalancing is simply the side-to-side tilting of the upper body at the waist in the direction opposite the turn or change in direction as shown in figure 3.7. If you have trouble turning with speed or keeping the skis or board on edge through the turn, you should concentrate on learning how to make proper counterbalancing movements. The signature of good counterbalancing is a still or calm upper body with the hips, legs, knees, and ankles moving side to side under the torso.

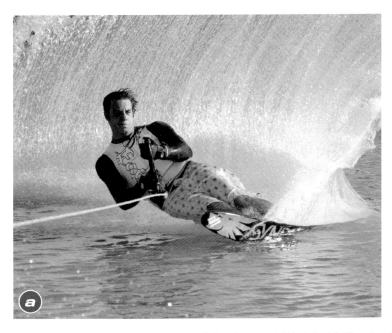

Figure 3.7   Counterbalancing on a *(a)* slalom and *(b)* trick ski. The shoulders tilt in the opposite direction of the ski.

Figure 3.8 **Fore–aft balance keeps you in a balanced position relative to the pull of the boat.**

Fore–aft balance movements are in response to the location of the hips relative to the feet. Think of your feet on the skis or board as being between your hips and the boat (see figure 3.8). This position or body alignment requires an overall body tension. A break down in that alignment and tension is often one of the first signs that you are getting tired. Rather than focusing on moving the hips to maintain fore–aft balance, focus on moving the feet. Fore–aft balance is most critical during the initiation of a change of direction and just before the rope is reloaded and stretched. The movement is initiated by the foot nearer the boat and acts to center the body over the skis or board. Fore–aft movement combined with flexing and extending create what is called upper-body/lower-body separation in snow skiing; the same principle applies on the water. Keep your upper body calm and keep your movement below the hips.

Counteracting for Rotation

Counteracting movements are some of the least understood and most difficult to teach. Many coaches will tell you not to move your upper body but to keep it still to help maintain balance. However, if your upper body does not move, you limit the amount of edge tipping you can establish. This means less control of speed and change of direction. Proper counteracting movements are the answer.

Counteracting movements occur in the direction opposite of what is happening with the lower body. As with tipping, counteracting may be subtle or quite strong, and active or reactive depending on the speed and amount of rotation desired. The countering movement establishes stable and strong edge contact and balance by creating skeletal alignment that works with the design of the skis or board to efficiently change direction and advance before loading the ski and rope.

The amount of counteracting should always be in correlation with and equal to the amount of direction change required; counteracting should not be done to such an extent that it affects balance on the water. A proper counteracting movement augments the grip of the skis or board and allows for stronger tipping movements and flexion with more acute angles. The counteracting movements also stack the legs and hip in alignment to resist the push of the turn created by centrifugal force.

To enhance counteracting for rotation, the movements need to occur at the initiation of the change in direction with a turn of the torso or shoulders away from the direction of the turn as shown in figure 3.9. You turn torso or shoulders in the direction opposite of the turn while keeping your hips, ankles, and knees

Figure 3.9 Counteracting movements load your body and ski for a turn or rotation.

in a neutral position, and then you turn the torso and shoulders into to the turn. This movement essentially serves as a wind up that gives you the force you need to create rotation. Focus on keeping the tipping of the skis or board and the counteracting movement in sync. Also, concentrate on the direction rather than the distance of the counteracting movement.

A skillful performance on the water is the result of an awareness of how to make movements correctly. Chapter 8 is devoted to specific off- and on-water drills to help you feel these movements so you can develop good balance and body position on the water. Learning these movements will help you interpret and respond better to factors such as wind and water conditions, assess the performance of your equipment, and determine the movements that are best suited for the situation.

When it all comes together, you will experience moments of excellence. Those moments are the result of countless hours of preparation coming together to create that performance. It is the culmination of the 25 percent rule. The time spent on strength and conditioning, testing and tweaking equipment to make it ideal, and perfecting the moves and techniques of the sport, combined with learning how to compete when the pressure on, is time well spent.

The Future of the Biomechanics of Water Sports

We understand the movements and motions of the record holders. What we don't know is precisely when and how much of each movement you must apply to perform a specific task. For example, what is the exact angle of approach and the exact amount of lift and speed needed for performing a flip? Kinematics has been traditionally studied qualitatively and quantitatively via high-speed video. Kinetic analysis has traditionally involved load cells, strain gauges, and force platforms. Measurement involves the design, construction, and use of sophisticated instruments that can measure time, position, velocity, acceleration, force, torque, temperature, and many other factors. Unfortunately, the data for our sport are weak at best in this area. Although attempts have been made and much information has been gathered, it seems no one has been able to convert the data into usable, actionable information.

We need these data to help athletes and coaches "see better." Advancements in X-rays, MRIs, PET scans, infrared thermographs, and many other technologies have helped us see better. Biomechanics applies many of these technologies to sport. Compared to most Olympic-level sports, however, water skiing and wakeboarding have not made good use of biomechanics. The USOCs for snow skiing, swimming, track, gymnastics, and many other sports have developed systems that use high-speed video and computer digitization to render athlete performance in two or three dimensions and to produce extremely precise measurements of athlete motion while training and competing. They have also built custom timing systems that can render times accurately to 1/1,000th of a second for almost any performance.

Custom sensing equipment allows coaches and athletes to see the most subtle aspects of performance such as oar forces and positions in a rowing shell; the position, speed, and force of the barbell in weightlifting; and accelerations of and forces on a standard punching bag for boxing and taekwondo. Electromyography is used to analyze muscle electrical activity and to determine whether learning drills and skills are muscularly similar to the real skill, or whether an athlete's injured muscle has returned to levels comparable to those of noninjured muscles. New magnetic field generators and sensors obtain information about motion in six dimensions in real time (while the athlete is actually performing, and therefore with no delay for data processing) allowing a computer to generate a robot image that moves precisely the same way the athlete moves. The computerized robot can be programmed to provide audible feedback tones when the athlete is in a specific position or range of positions. Thus, the athlete can see herself perform as the robot, while the specific body positions, speeds, and angles can be preprogrammed so the computer tells the athlete when she's doing it right and when she's doing it wrong.

A new video-overlay system allows pertinent physical and physiological data to be placed on a video image of a performance so that coaches and athletes can see them at the same time. Special force-sensing equipment allows coaches and athletes to see their force and power performances in subtle but important ways and in real time using high-speed video so that rapid movements can be slowed down and studied in clear slow motion.

All of this is needed for water skiing and wakeboarding. Today we use standard video sporadically, and it is often incapable of resolving the more subtle aspects of performance that are only visible with high-speed cameras. Biomechanics of the future is not just about technique. The field has expanded its reach to many areas that open new horizons for athletes to see better, understand better, and thereby perform better.

Chapter 4

Slalom Skiing

ike many slalom skiers, the first thing that grabbed my attention about the event was the massive wall of water a good slalom skier launches into the air on a turn. As a kid growing up in Covington, Louisiana, I remember watching a guy behind a yellow Galaxy inboard/outboard on his EP Comp 2 putting up a spray that seemed to go over the top of the pine and cypress trees lining the Tchefuncte River. Making as big a spray as possible was all that mattered to me. The size of the spray established the pecking order for skill and reputation on the river, and my friends and I all wanted to be the king of the river—that is, until we were introduced to the rhythm, power, and precision of slalom skiing. Whether your goal is to be king or queen of the river or to run rope lengths in the slalom course in competition, this chapter provides the skills, drills, and learning progressions to get you there.

Body Position

The first thing you need to be able to do to create big spray or run the slalom course is cross the wakes in a stable, balanced, and strong position. Without a doubt, this is the most important part of slalom skiing. Learning to establish and maintain your direction across the wakes (or "hold angle," as slalom skiers call it) is a simple three-step process.

1. Practice on Land or in the Boat

On land, tie a handle to a post or a door, or in the boat, tie a handle to the pylon, and practice getting into proper slalom position (see figure 4.1). The head and eyes are parallel to the water (or ground), *the arms are straight,* the knees and ankles are considerably flexed, the handle is away from the hips, and the hips are dropped away from the handle. Hold this position for a minute or so, and feel where the pull, or strain, is. It should be in your legs and feet, and to a lesser extent in your upper back and shoulders. After holding this position for a minute, do the same thing pointing in the other direction. To get tension in your legs and feet, open your hips and shoulders more toward the handle. The pros do this drill to wake up their muscles before a run. Practice this drill frequently to build the muscles and balance needed for holding direction across the wakes. The stronger and more confident you are in this position, the easier slalom will be.

Figure 4.1 **Learning a comfortable and balanced stance on land builds the correct foundation for slalom.**

2. Practice Behind the Boat

Now it's time to do the drill on the water. Shorten the rope to 28 off (the yellow loop). This will take away the slack rope feeling and keep the rope tight during the drill. Have the driver run the boat at about 24 to 28 mph (39 to 45 km/h) for an adult (slower for children). Position yourself at the base of the wake. While riding there, shift into the correct body position. Get your head up, extend your arms out straight, bring your hips to the handle, and bend your knees and ankles. Spot a point on the shore on your side of the wake and start leaning toward it. Hold that position until you are as far up on this side of the boat as you can get. Maintain the position down the full length of the lake. After you turn around, repeat the drill on the other side of the boat. You will likely find that maintaining the position (see figure 4.2) is easier on one side than the other. Your on side and off side are usually determined by which foot you put forward in your ski. The secret is to get comfortable and confident on both sides.

Figure 4.2 **Being able to hold the correct body position with proper alignment and balance on the water is critical to learning slalom.**

3. Cross the Wakes

You now have all of the skills and, most important, the correct body alignment required to slice right through those bumps of water behind the boat. With the rope still at the yellow loop, start at the base of the wake, as you did in step 2. Get into your newly developed perfect body alignment, tip the ski and lean until you are 20 feet (6 m) outside the wake. Then, go into a brief glide with your ski flat on the water's surface and set yourself into proper position. As you begin to slow down, but before you get pulled back toward the wake as the rope tightens, make a slow transition, or tip your ski (see figure 4.3), in the opposite direction

Figure 4.3 **Learning to tip and edge across the wakes.**

(toward the wake) and lock yourself into correct body alignment. Start off in an easy ski tip and lean through the wake the same way you did on the side of the boat. As you make the turn toward the wake, remember to keep your head up and look across to a point on the shore. Keep leaning through the wake until you are all the way up alongside the boat as in step 2. Come out of your lean and off your edge, and now make a slow turn and head back the other way. Get a bit more aggressive each time you go across, and focus on balance and speed control while tipping the ski onto its edge. Keep practicing. This drill takes time to perfect, but once you get it down, learning to run the course is a breeze.

The following checklist will help you achieve proper body position and lean:

- Keep your arms straight! Think about leaning against the rope with your arms relaxed.
- Flex your knees more and keep them active.
- Drop your hips away from the handle, and feel the tension in your feet and shoulders.
- Keep your ski tipped, and edge so the ski can cut through the wakes rather than riding over them. If you get pulled to a flat ski as you approach the wakes, start with a less aggressive tip of the ski, and focus on keeping the ski tipped and on edge when approaching the wakes.
- Keep your upper body calm and still. The only body parts that move through the wakes are the knees. The idea is to lock out the upper body and shift the stress and strain of the boat's pull to your strongest muscles, your legs. This transfers the energy of the boat efficiently to the ski. You can think of it as tug of war in which you push with your legs rather than pull with your arms to create leverage and lean.

Running the Slalom Course

You have now mastered the fundamental skills needed for learning how to run the slalom course. You have proper body alignment and balance and can control your speed and direction across the wakes while maintaining your body position. This is when the real fun begins. The rocketlike acceleration; the tight, gripping turns; and the adrenaline rush of controlled speed are what make slalom so addictive. The slalom course provides an added bonus, too: the constant challenge to improve. You can always learn another rope length. Skiers get mesmerized by the slalom course, constantly looking for a new and better way to run that next pass or get to that extra buoy. The lure and challenge of slalom skiing begins by learning how to run the minicourse, then continues as you run the narrow course and, finally, the full slalom course.

Minicourse

The minicourse is simply half of the full slalom course. The boat is driven down the right side of the course between the boat guide buoys on the left and the skier turn buoys on the right (see figure 4.4). The driver should start at 20 to

26 mph (32 to 42 km/h) for adults and hold the speed constant. The rope should be at the first or second loop (red or orange). Get in the correct body position, and pull out to the right side of the boat, about 25 feet (40 km/h). As buoy 1 approaches, make a smooth tip of the ski on the left edge (closer to the boat) and ski around the buoy, finishing the turn so you are skiing across the course as you pass the downcourse side of the buoy. Here comes the critical part: You must maintain correct body position, lean against the handle, and hold direction without breaking your body position through both wakes.

As you ski across the wakes, look 20 feet (6 m) in front of the next buoy (the left boat guide buoy). Once across the second wake, change your edge with a tip of the ski back to the right and let the ski make a smooth turn around buoy 2 and back across the course (see figure 4.5). Repeat the process across the wakes; keep your head up, arms straight, and knees flexed; and lean across the wakes looking to a point in front of buoy 3. Make another smooth turn and head for buoy 4. Again, lean through the wakes, turn, and lean again to buoy 5 and then buoy 6. You did it! You have taken your first steps to becoming a slalom god.

Keep running the minicourse until you can make it at about 26 to 30 mph (42 to 48 km/h) depending on your skill, size, and weight. Remember to focus on the lean through the wakes and maintaining correct body position and balance. The minicourse teaches you the rhythm of slalom that is vital for running the big course. An important thing to note here is that the slalom course and even minicourse are about making six turns and six pulls. Rarely do skiers, even the world's best, make six perfect turns and pulls. You need to be a fighter; never give up on a pass unless you miss a buoy or fall. When you have a bobble or break out of proper position, *do not quit!* Make a strong lean or a hard turn, and get back into the pass. You will be amazed at the number of buoys you will run when you keep fighting and refuse to give up.

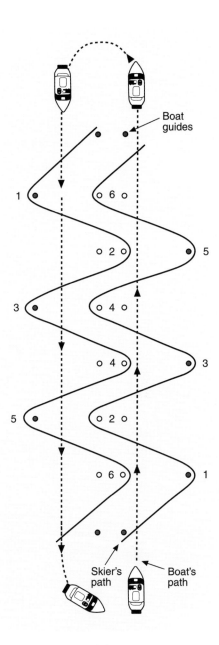

Figure 4.4 The minicourse.

Figure 4.5 Turning around the boat guide buoy on the minicourse.

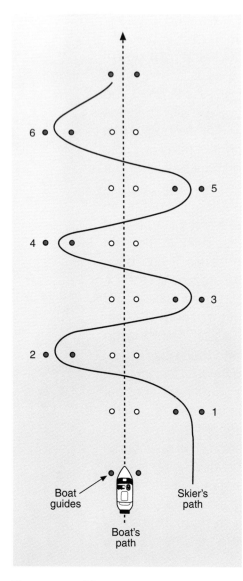

Figure 4.6   The narrow course.

Narrow Course

The narrow course (also known as the shadow course) is the same as the regular course except that the buoys are 10 feet (3 m) closer to the boat (see figure 4.6) than the buoys in the regular course. If you don't have a narrow course, just drop some buoys in or imagine that there is another set of buoys in place inside the regular skier buoys.

Have the driver go through the boat guide buoys at 24 to 28 mph (39 to 45 km/h). This may feel slow, but if you are tipping and in a balanced, aligned position, you will generate plenty of speed to carry you through the turns. Start with the rope at either long line (75 feet, or 23 m) or 15 off (the first cut loop, red). I recommend pulling out all the way outside the first full-course buoy, even though you will be running the narrow course to help build strength and balance from that position. Get yourself at least 3 feet (1 m) wide of the first buoy and start the turn 10 feet (3 m) before the buoy, as you did on the minicourse, so you can finish the turn on the backside of the buoy. From there, it is five more turns, six leans, and out the exit gates.

As in the minicourse, your turns need to be smooth and slow, and you need strong, powerful alignment and balance through the wakes. The emphasis remains on holding your direction across the wakes to give you plenty of time to make a smooth, controlled transition into the next turn. Resist the pull from the boat, especially at the second wake, by driving your shoulder that is farther from the boat down and back and away from the boat as you cross the wakes. Doing so will help you hold the angle and lean longer, giving you acceleration if you are losing speed in the turns. Because you are skiing from a wider position, you may have a tendency to generate your angle too soon and get pulled up at the wakes. The solution is to have a progressive lean with your greatest resistance through the wakes. When you get across the wakes and are waiting for the next buoy, get into the habit of staying down in your ski with your knees and ankles flexed. Remember to start your turns well before the oncoming buoy. I like to simplify slalom to just a turn and a lean. Don't try to think of a preturn; just lean through both wakes, change direction in your turn, and lean the other way.

Full Course

The primary difference between the full course (see figure 4.7) and the mini-course or narrow course is the intensity level. The fundamentals are the same:

- Body position is critical: keep your arms straight, knees and ankles flexed, hips away from the handle, and head and eyes parallel with the horizon.
- Hold your alignment, balance, and direction through both wakes and especially at the second wake.
- Establish a rhythm in your turn and lean.
- Most important, never give up on a pass!

The easiest way to learn to run the full course is to start by skiing wide of buoy 1 as you did with the narrow course. Then shadow buoys 2, 3, 4, and 5. When you lean from buoy 5 to buoy 6, keep leaning until you get on the outside of buoy 6. Once you can do this successfully, start skiing around buoy 5, and then work to become proficient with this pattern. Each time you succeed, add another buoy until you can ski around all six buoys. Before you know it, you will run a complete pass.

Turns

Most skiers focus on the turn because that is where the big spray is generated. The real secret to slalom, though, is creating angle and holding it through the wakes with correct body position (see figure 4.8).

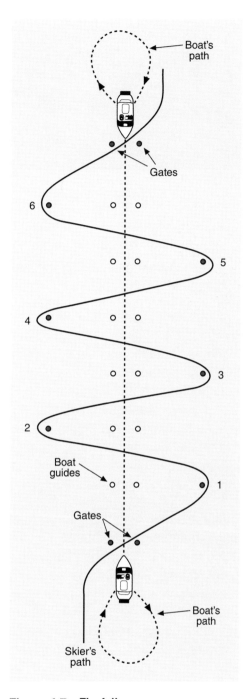

Figure 4.7 **The full course.**

Most people do the turns naturally once they learn to keep the ski tipped and on edge across the wakes. Slalom gets very complicated when you break down every movement. An easier approach is to keep it simple and spend time concentrating on body position through the wakes, and think of the turn as a simple change of direction. Following are three things you should think about in the turns:

1. The edge change should be quick and smooth and initiated with the ankles, knees, and hips. Stay down in your ski with your knees and ankles flexed to maintain speed through the turn.

Figure 4.8 The key to slalom is learning to hold direction across wakes and across the course.

2. Reach with the handle to the side toward the boat and slightly up to keep your head and chest still and calm in the turn.

3. Let the ski pass under the rope. Start tipping the ski into your lean when you see the ski move between you and the boat.

From there, you simply set your ski angle across the course and hold that direction. Two-handed turns are beneficial because they force you to use knee flexion and teach you how to control the rope and stay with the rhythm and timing of the boat, rope, and course. You should begin using one-handed turns only after you can run the course with two hands at 15 off and 30 mph (48 km/h). Do whatever it takes to make six buoys every time you enter the course. When you have learned the rhythm of making six turns and leans in the confines of the slalom course, you are ready to conquer the gates and begin working on developing consistency, strength, and timing in your skiing.

Gates

Every pro tour skier will tell you that the gates are the key to every pass. Good gates mean a good first buoy, and that sets you up for the rest of the pass. Yet, there is so much inconsistency and debate around how slalom skiers do and teach gates. Whether you do a one-handed West Coast–style gate or a two-handed old school–style gate, the objective is the same: to consistently get maximum crosscourse direction and angle at the right-hand-gate buoy to set you up for a good first buoy. For either type of gate, you must know the answers to five questions to achieve consistently good gates:

1. **Where should you position yourself behind the boat before you pull out?** The answer is that it does not matter, but you should be in the same position each time. The next time you ski, when you are getting ready to pull out for the gate, see if you are at the base of the wake, just outside the foam or spray from the boat, or behind the boat. Even better, look downcourse at the boat guides and see whether you are inside or outside of them. Boats have many variations of spray, troughs, and wakes, but the course is always the same. Positioning yourself in relation to the boat guides is the most consistent pullout method.

2. **When should you start the pullout for the entrance gates?** The pregate buoys are the best reference point to determine when to start your pullout

for the entrance gates. Look to see where you or the boat is located in relation to the pregates when you start your pullout. In the West Coast style, the pregates should appear from behind the boat as the boat travels through them and just past you before you begin the pullout. For old school gates, you usually pull out just as the boat approaches or goes into the gates, depending on your speed and your rope length. There is not a right or wrong answer to this question; you just need to have a keen awareness of when to start your pullout to get consistently good gates.

3. **How hard should you pull out?** How hard you pull out, or the intensity of the lean, controls your acceleration up alongside the boat as well as how long you glide next to the boat. This determines how hard and when you will need to turn to get a good gate. You also want to know where you pull with the most intensity. If you pull hard to start and easier at the end, you will lose speed quickly. If you have a more progressive pullout with more intensity at the end, you will have more forward speed and glide time. Again, the key is developing awareness so you can have reproducible gates regardless of the circumstance.

4. **When should you stop your pullout?** The point at which you stop your pullout controls how wide you will be for your turn toward the entrance into the gates. You can use the 2-4-6 buoy line, the position of the boat in relation to the entrance gates, or (my favorite) the alignment of the left-hand entrance gate and buoy 3 to decide when to stop the pullout and go into a glide. The angle of the rope on the side of the boat is also a great reference point. The patented SmartStart system, developed by slalom aficionado, Mark Bozicevic, uses marks on the side of the boat and offers a direct, consistent visual cue to help develop a reproducible gate position.

5. **When should you start the turn toward the entrance gates?** This is the most difficult of the five questions because it changes at different speed and rope lengths. Nevertheless, you should use the same visual cues or triggers as a reference and adjust the timing to get good gates. Look to see where the boat is when you start your turn. Are the entrance gates touching the bow, or coming out past the platform? You can also look at the relationship between the left-hand-gate buoy and the first-turn ball as a cue (see figure 4.9). No matter what style of gate you use, you must always be moving slightly faster than the boat when you make your turn for the gate so your ski has time to change direction and get in front of you before you begin holding direction. You initiate the turn for the gate with a tip of the ski, which starts with your knees pointing toward the right-hand gate; your upper body follows.

Once you know the answers to these questions, you will be able to perform consistently and make adjustments. If you are in a slump and not skiing as well as you think you should be, or if you are not progressing or falling after only a few buoys, more than likely you are not performing the correct start. Go back to question 1 to see whether you are pulling out correctly before messing with anything else in your skiing technique or equipment.

Figure 4.9 Referencing the imaginary line between the left gate buoy and buoy 1 is a great way to help you determine when to turn for the gate.

If you nailed the gate shot and all of your visual cues on the gate, you can simply make a smooth, controlled turn just as you did when you were pulling out for buoy 1 to learn how to run the course. Now it's time to get back into position and start your lean to buoy 2. But sometimes it's not that simple. The distance from the gates to buoy 1 is shorter than any other segment of the course, and because of this, handle control becomes critical. Handle control requires keeping the handle in close to your body and low, between your hips and knees. By doing this through the lean, you maintain your angle and direction across the wakes, and your shoulders and ski move in the same direction. The load, or pressure, forced on your ski will aid you in the edge change. The other part of handle control is holding on to the handle with both hands until you are into your turn, outside of the buoy line, and beyond 32 off, or the green loop of the rope. Good handle control will help you ski wide of the buoy so you can make your turn on the backside of the buoy and have more time to set up each subsequent turn. The turn should be a smooth, quick change of direction initiated by a tip of the ski that sets you up for a powerful lean through the wakes to buoy 2.

Learning the Next Pass

Running the full slalom course for the first time will give you a feeling of personal triumph. You may come out of the gates, throw up the iron fist, and let out a scream of joy. After a few times making the course you will start craving that feeling of victory over the course again. Learning the next pass is a new challenge. You create this challenge by increasing the speed of the boat or by shortening the rope. Either change requires you to increase your intensity, focus, and skill. You may try and try on this new pass, but nothing works. You may get slack at one ball, you may not be able to get the gates right, you may not be able to get into a lean behind the boat, or you may keep overturning or falling at the buoy. The secret to learning the next pass is to use an organized and structured approach rather than trying to imitate the pros or using random drills and techniques. The steps mapped out in the following sections will help you learn the next speed or line length. They will also help you build strength and consistency in your slalom skiing.

Learn the Pass in Parts

Learning the pass in parts is a great way to progress rapidly from your learning speed to the maximum speed for your age or gender group. It also works just as well for short-line passes. At faster speeds and shorter rope lengths, the pull is quicker and much more intense, making the gates even more critical and difficult to nail. The best plan is to learn a new pass the same way you learned your first pass, by skipping the gates at first. Break each new pass into two sections: the rhythm of the pass and the gate. First, learn the rhythm of the pass by making six buoys. Then, go back to learn the gate you need to get into position on the course. In one day, this approach has taught pros how to run 39 off. It can also help rookies learn two and three passes in a day.

1. **The rhythm of the pass.** Time your turn and lean through the gates so you ski 5 feet (1.5 m) outside of the right-hand gate. Use the same gate cues and system you learned with the five questions, but just do it about 10 feet (3 m) earlier to miss the gates on the early side. This will position you wide on buoy 1 and give you ample time to slow down to make a nice, smooth turn on the backside of the buoy. Now you are off and running the pass. From there on, you simply need to learn how to hold the additional stress of the pull from the boat. Focus on maintaining your body alignment and crosscourse direction above all else. Once you have a feel for the pass, you are ready to add the gate into the equation.

2. **The gate.** Once you can run the pass by missing the gates by 5 feet (1.5 m), do the same thing, but miss them by 2 feet (0.6 m). Just start your gate routine a bit later than you did before, and as always, hold your lean and angle through the gates and maintain handle control out to the buoy. Once you can run the pass from a 2-foot miss position, go for the whole thing. Stay focused. You know you can run the pass once you get started. If you get the perfect gate and buoy 1 and fall at buoy 2 or 3, stay calm. Most likely, you are coming to buoy 2 still thinking about that awesome gate and buoy 1 you just had rather than changing direction for buoy 2. Then, just like that, you are in the water. Once you develop the consistency on the gate, the pass will be a snap, but break the pass up into the rhythm and the gate shot to get to the pass going.

Speed It Up

Once you get to the top speed of your division and are trying shorter rope lengths, you may feel as though the boat is moving faster. It's not; you are. As the rope gets shorter, the physics of slalom are such that you now travel a greater distance in the same amount of time. The shorter the rope, the quicker things happen in the course. You need to edge change, turn, and get into your lean more quickly and efficiently. Prepare for this increase in acceleration by first running your current pass at a quarter to half mile per hour (or km/h) faster. These small increases in speed make things happen more quickly and increase the pull as well, requiring more strength and intensity to maintain your crosscourse direction and body position. This will sharpen your reflexes and get you ready for increased speeds at even shorter rope lengths.

Slow It Down

Once you are making passes at your maximum speed for your age and gender group and are battling it out with the next loop on the rope, try slowing the boat down in 1 mph (or km/h) increments until you can successfully run the pass with or without the gates. Once you make the pass and the gates and have a good feel for where you need to be on the course, how long you need to hold direction, and the intensity and timing of the pass, bump up the speed in 1 mph (or km/h) increments until you can run the pass at the correct speed or maximum speed for your age division.

Use a Midloop

Some drivers weave the boat closer to the skier turn buoys to help a skier stretching to make a new pass. I don't like this method because driving straight and staying in rhythm with the skier is hard enough; when you weave, things are even more inconsistent. I prefer a midloop. Using a midloop requires either adding a new loop in your rope between the pass you are currently running and the new pass, or wrapping the rope around the pylon a few times to shorten it just a bit. You can also buy ropes with premade midloops. Because the change isn't as dramatic with midloops, they can help you gain confidence and have a smooth transition into the new pass.

Choose Your Style

The bottom line when picking a style is to find one that works for you, whether it is West Coast, new school, old school, compression, angulation, inclination, stacking, or some other style. There is no right or wrong style; I can point to great skiers for every style. Your choice of style depends on your body type (tall or short, heavy or light, strong or weak, flexible or not as flexible), your equipment setup, and your understanding of the style you are trying to ski. This last point is important because you must examine each style to determine if your body, vision, and mindset fit the style.

Far too many skiers choose a particular style because they think it looks cool or they want to emulate a skier who uses that style. Even worse is the underinformed coach who is dedicated to a style and truly believes it is the only style for all slalom skiers. Saying there is only one slalom style is like saying there is only one way to swing a golf club or hit a tennis ball. Some fundamentals, such as getting the ski to maintain direction, are true for any style, but the final result still depends on your personal physical, mental, and technical abilities as well as your equipment.

Building Strength and Consistency

The paradox of slalom is that you get to your hardest passes when you are most tired. For this reason, a critical element of slalom training is to prepare you so you have maximum power and strength when you get to your most difficult pass. You must also make sure that you get to your most difficult pass often so you can press your limits and improve your scores. To do so, spend time developing and perfecting your fundamentals with the following drills.

Drill 1: Back to Backs

Back to backs are simply starting at your opening pass and running it as many times as you can without stopping the boat. Have the driver spin the boat at the end of the course and come back in. Start by running two or three passes and build up to more. Set a goal for yourself, or play a game with your training partner. When my coach, Jay Bennett, first instructed me to run back to backs, I did not see how running all those 28 and 32 off passes would help my high-end passes at 38 and 39 off. I soon learned that these drills were challenging and some of the best conditioning I did. Also, the benefits were innumerable. Back to backs build strength as a result of volume, improve your consistency through repetition, and bolster your confidence because you learn to ski in any conditions, to pull out of all sorts of bad situations, and to efficiently transfer the power of the boat to your ski.

Drill 2: Slow Skiing

The slow skiing drill was made famous by Kris LaPoint. It teaches you flawless body position and the importance of pulling hard and strong through both wakes. Run your first or second pass and have the driver stop the boat. Shorten the rope to 15 or 22 off (shorter if you are an advanced skier). Now have the driver go through the course at 2 mph (3.2 km/h) slower than your normal speed. Have the driver spin the boat and come back in 2 mph (3.2 km/h) slower than before. Keeping doing this until you are going as slowly as you can. You will find that you must exaggerate everything (body position, lean) to make the pass. The smallest mistake puts you in the drink, so stay strong and work it.

Drill 3: Seventh Buoy

"What? There are only six buoys in the course," you may say. That's true. In this drill you set out or imagine a seventh buoy and make a turn at buoy 6 just as you do at buoys 2 and 4. Having the extra turn and lean keeps you from getting lazy at buoy 5 or buoy 6 and prevents the "I got this pass run" mentality from popping up because it's not over until you are around buoy 7. Turn at buoy 7 and go back through the pregates.

Drill 4: Two Handing

Now that you are a veteran slalom course skier and are making perfect wide, sweeping one-hand reaches and turns, try to run a pass with two hands on the handle in the turns, just as you did when you were first learning. It's harder than you may think. This drill breaks up the turn and lean into two separate phases and teaches you handle control. Steve Schnitzer, several-time national champion and slalom technical innovator, is the best two hander I've ever seen. Schnitz is an amazing technical skier, and I've seen him run 38 off two handed. A few pointers for this drill are to keep your chest up in the turn and the ski in front of you by staying down in your ski. Also, after finishing the turn, make a strong lean to make up time. This drill will teach you how to get across the wakes quickly. Finally, reach with your outside hand. Begin by having the driver slow the boat down 2 mph (3.2 km/h) the first time you try two handing; then build back up and see how far you can go.

Slalom Theory—Pendulum Effect and Skiing Early

Understanding the pendulum effect will help you with slalom skiing. In slalom, you are like the weight that moves back and forth at the end of a pendulum staff. You must maintain your momentum, angle, and direction through the wakes and into the edge change by keeping your shoulders traveling across the course, rather than letting them rotate back toward the boat. If you feel a burst of speed off the second wake, that's OK. This extra resistance at the second wake will allow you to ski out wider of the buoy and slow you down so you finish the turn on the backside of the buoy. If you don't ski wide of the buoy, you will carry too much speed down the course. Skiing wide enables you to finish the turn at the buoy and move farther up alongside of the boat so you can get into the acceleration and lean phase sooner. The sooner you lean, the quicker you will get to the other side of the course and the earlier you will be at the next buoy. If you are narrow or late in the slalom course, think wide and employ the pendulum effect.

Another important aspect of slalom theory is skiing early, which means to create distance and time between you and the next turn buoy. When you nail that turn and get the great feeling of angle on the backside of the buoy, the temptation is to look across the course, see how early you are going to be, and forget the lean. I call this skiing lazy. Learn to suppress the elation that comes from a great turn; you still have a lot of work to do. Take all of that angle you have created and turn it into acceleration as quickly as possible to get to the other side of the course. Pull your hardest as you approach the spray and across the wakes (see figures 4.10 and 4.11) because in this situation you have the correct direction and angle. This will position you farther up alongside the boat and prevents the boat from pulling you forward in the turn.

Figure 4.10 The hardest part of a lean begins at the spray (white water) and across the wakes.

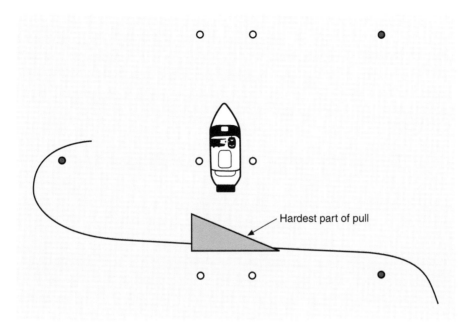

Figure 4.11 **Your hardest pull should be behind the boat.**

If you feel you are being pulled forward over the ski, you are behind the boat or chasing the boat in the turn. When you fail to attain your angle out of the turn, you need to pull your hardest as quickly as you can (see figure 4.12). You still have a chance to create angle before the wakes because you are still up on the boat a bit, so get your shoulders rotated and lean. In this situation, you need to

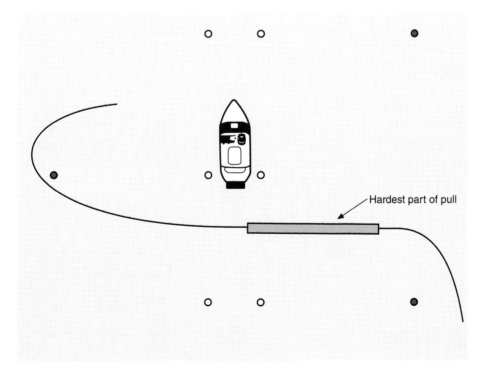

Figure 4.12 **If you don't have the proper angle out of the turn, you can still create angle before the wakes by pulling your hardest as quickly as you can.**

pull your hardest as soon as you get both hands back on the handle, before the first wake. You must then maintain your pull and angle through the wakes and be patient at the next buoy because you will be a little narrow still and a little fast. The good news is that you have another chance to make up more time in the next pull. Don't try to run a pass with one turn or pull; stay in the pass and on your ski. Work with the pass and never give up.

Selecting and Tuning Your Slalom Ski

Few skiers ever find the optimum equipment setup. Most seem to be stuck at the extremes of the continuum. Either they spend nearly all their time fiddling with fin settings or ski adjustments, or they are scared to touch their ski setup for fear of losing what feels good. The problem with not trying new skis or settings is that you never know whether there is a better ski or a better setup that will help you overcome your faults. To advance your skiing scores, try the following tips for selecting a ski and setting it up.

Selecting a New Ski

Before buying, get several demo skis from your local pro shop. Look for skis that will build on your strengths and help correct your weaknesses. If you have great turns and poor pulls, try skis that are known for getting across the wakes with good angle. If you are a bull across the wakes, but have trouble slowing down and turning, try skis with better deceleration and turning characteristics. Rate each ski on turning, acceleration, deceleration, and maintaining angle across the wakes. Consider what each demo ski does differently (both better and worse) from your current ski, and then make a decision based on those answers, not the colors or price. Remember that the only benefit of a ski that feels the same as your old one is newer graphics.

Once you find a ski that you like and that works for you, spend a few sets adjusting to it before making any setup changes. Once you are comfortable riding the ski and know what it can do, begin fine-tuning the setup. Start with the bindings, then the fin, and as a last measure, take out the file or sandpaper to dial it in. This is where you need to be careful and track each change. Make only one change at a time, and take notes on what you changed and how it affected the ski's performance. You should also make sure you are not inadvertently causing the problems you are encountering by skiing lazy or tired. Remember, every adjustment will improve one aspect of the ski's performance, but only at the cost of making another characteristic less than perfect. Once you get into the season, have confidence in your setup so you do not fall into the trap of overtuning your ski so you can spend your time skiing rather than constantly fiddling with your ski setup.

Tuning Your Ski

A variety of design elements determine the personality, or performance characteristics, of a slalom ski. A change in any of these elements totally changes the attitude of the ski and affects the other components and attributes, as well as its performance. Remember that no one ski design is best. You must find a ski that works for you and helps you overcome your technical flaws. Everything in ski design is a trade-off. When you increase one characteristic, you decrease another. Find what works for you through experimentation. Following are descriptions of each of the ski personality and performance elements and the effects they have on a ski, as well explanations of how to tune or adjust them.

Binding Location   The first adjustment to look at is your binding position. I recommend the binding locations set at the factory, but there is always the temptation to move them forward or backward a notch or two. Some people drill new holes in the ski to get the bindings to a location they believe will work. The on-side turn (buoys 2, 4, and 6 for right-foot-forward skiers and buoys 1, 3, and 5 for left-foot-forward skiers) is controlled by your rear foot. The off-side turn is controlled by your front foot. The following guidance will help you decide whether you need to move your bindings.

Forward—Moving your bindings forward gives you quicker deceleration and tighter turns. You are too far forward if you ski narrow and reach forward.

Backward—Moving your bindings backward gives you better acceleration and makes you commit to the turn. You are too far back if the ski will not slow down and you have to put excessive weight on your front foot to slow the ski down.

Bottom Design   Manufacturers use three bottom designs (see figure 4.13). Try different tunnel designs to find one that matches the way you ski or want a ski to perform.

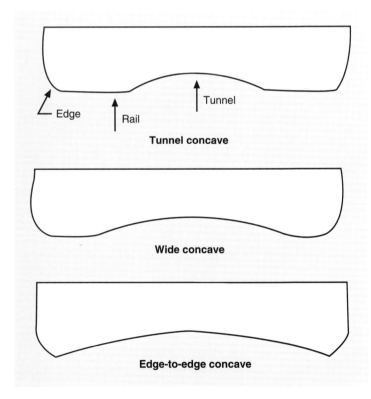

Figure 4.13   Bottom designs include the *(a)* tunnel concave, *(b)* wide concave, and *(c)* edge-to-edge concave.

Tunnel concave—Narrow concave tunnels are more stable and track better than other tunnels. If the rails are angled toward the bevel, the ski will roll on edge more easily. Rails provide lift and stability.

Wide concave—Wide concave skis sit deeper, change edges easier, and are less stable on the water than other styles of skis. Deeper concave skis decelerate and hold better crosscourse direction. Shallower concave skis ride higher on the water, which makes them easier to turn.

Edge-to-edge—Edge-to-edge concave skis have increased surface area in the tunnel, which gives them more suction and holding power than other skis.

Edge Shape   Skis have one of two types of bevels (see figure 4.14). The greater the size of the bevel, the farther the ski will drop down into the water, resulting in a steadier ride with more drag. The smaller the bevel, the higher the ski will ride on the water.

45-degree bevel—Sharp edges lift the ski higher, resulting in less drag and less spray. The ski rides as though it were on a track or a rail.

Modified 45-degree bevel—The ski sits deeper in the water than a straight 45-degree bevel ski does, making it easier to turn, although it does not track as well. The rounder the bevel, the more the ski will drop into the water and the easier it will roll from edge to edge.

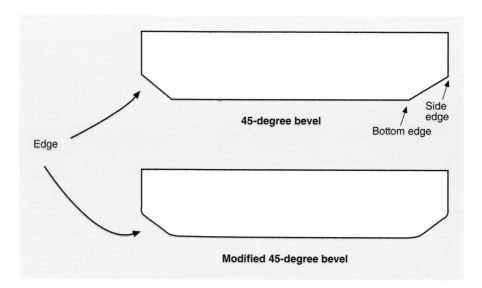

Figure 4.14   **Edge shapes include the *(a)* 45-degree bevel and the *(b)* modified 45-degree bevel.**

Little has been said or written about edge tuning since the 1975 article in *The Water Skier*, "How to Tune a Slalom Ski" by Dave Saucier (see table 4.1). The pros all fine tune the edges of their skis to get them set correctly, and for this reason Saucier's article is still the edge tuner's bible. You can change a lot by working edges, so proceed with caution when you start filing. Table 4.1 explains what to do in each of the three zones of a ski, which are shown in figure 4.15.

TABLE 4.1 Ski Tuning Troubleshooting Chart

Trouble	Zone	Soften	Sharpen	Bottom edge	Side edge
		Solution			
Ski lifts excessively over wake	1, 2	X		X	
Ski shifts edges slowly	2	X		X	
Ski is slow getting into preturn braking	2	X		X	
Ski lacks preturn aggression (preturn radius too large) during braking and extension	3	X		X	
Ski dumps too quickly (causes breaking at waist)	3		X		X
Ski dumps before pull-in and weight shift starts	3		X		X
Ski tip dives on bad side during washout	3[a]		X		X
Ski tip chatters during dump and washout	3		X		X
Ski tip lacks aggression during dump and washout; lays you down or requires excess body angle to get into proper acceleration path	2[b]	X		X	
Ski lacks track on acceleration; does not carve into wake	1[c]		X		X
Ski shoots out of course approaching bad side turn; actually turns wrong way as you start preturn (hard fall)	3[d]	X		X	
Ski walks or hunts from one side to another when going straight ahead (i.e., it wiggles)	2[e]				
Ski rides too high out of water overall	1,2[f]	X		X	
Ski rides at too shallow angle to direction of travel (i.e., tail is too high, tip too low)	1	X		X	
Lack of preturn braking coming around buoy into slack line even though you are in correct path	2	X		X	
Ski tends to bounce as it lands off wake; tends to rebound (two possible zones; two possible solutions)	1,2	X	X	X	X Forward part only
Ski jets out from under skier at 4th, 5th cuts (First, check finding location for being back too far or for ski being too short for skier's weight.)	1	X Greatly		X Just at fin area	
Ski seems slow on acceleration (i.e., attack angle too shallow)	2	X			X

[a]Possibly slightly wider bevel in this area.
[b]Favor point in between feet.
[c]Especially at fin area.
[d]Soften tunnel edges also full length.
[e]Zone of demarcation between two edges must be established; i.e., two edges have been softened into each other. Also check binding location. Bindings back too far (2 to 3 inches) cause this.
[f]Also increase bevel width and re-edge (both zones).

Adapted from D. Saucier, 1975 (Dec./Jan.), "How to tune a slalom ski," *The Water Skier*. Used with permission from USA Water Ski.

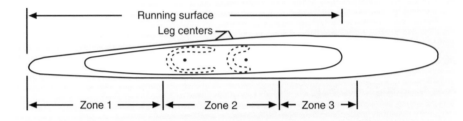

Figure 4.15 Ski tuning zones.

Adapted from D. Saucier, 1975 (Dec./Jan.), "How to tune a slalom ski," *The Water Skier*. Used with permission from USA Water Ski.

Perimeter Shape The following are the types of perimeter shapes you may encounter.

Wide forebody—The wide forebody shape allows you to stand on the front of the ski to carve a turn without being thrown out the front.

Narrow forebody—The narrow forebody shape keeps you off the front and helps the ski turn if you are on the tail.

Wide tail—A wide tail offers better acceleration if you tend to ride the tail of the ski.

Narrow tail—A narrow tail helps you slow down more quickly and ride deeper in the water.

Wide midsection—A ski with a wide midsection is easier to turn because it pivots on the flat section.

Side Cut Following are the three types of side cuts.

Sharp pivot point—A sharp pivot point allows the ski to turn sharply.

Medium pivot point—A ski with a medium pivot point combines a pivot point and a smooth perimeter shape.

Smooth pivot point—A ski with a smooth pivot point has no abrupt pivot point, just a smooth, rounded perimeter.

Flex Flex, which works in conjunction with rocker pattern, is a variable that has been significantly impacted by new carbon graphite ski layup materials and new design patterns. Different flex patterns can be used to balance ski torque or twisting, dampen ski vibration or chatter, and quicken the rebound recovery time after a turn. Adjusting the flex pattern by adding stiffness creates more rapid ski acceleration but makes the ski harder to turn. A soft-flex ski is easier to turn and more forgiving but does not shoot you across the wakes as quickly.

Rocker Pattern Ski companies are beginning to do more testing with rocker patterns to understand the relationship between rocker pattern and ski flex. There are two basic rocker patterns (see figure 4.16). The more rocker a ski has in the tail, the easier it is to turn, but the less acceleration it has. The less tail rocker a ski has, the harder it is to turn, but the better it accelerates.

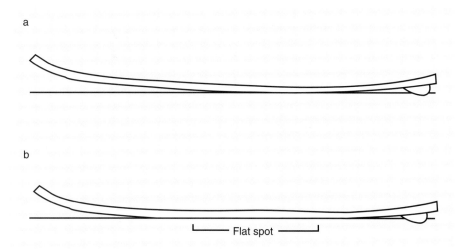

Figure 4.16 Rocker patterns may be *(a)* continuous or *(b)* flat section.

Continuous—A ski with a continuous rocker pattern is easier to turn when your weight is on the tail.

Flat section—This type of rocker pattern has a distinct tail with more rocker. It is more stable and accelerates better than a continuous pattern, and the flat section allows for weight to be distributed forward.

Fin Shape and Adjustment   You can choose from a variety of fin shapes (see figure 4.17).

Fins with flatter leading edges—These fins cause the front of the ski to stay up, resulting in more speed in the turn. They require more force to finish the turn.

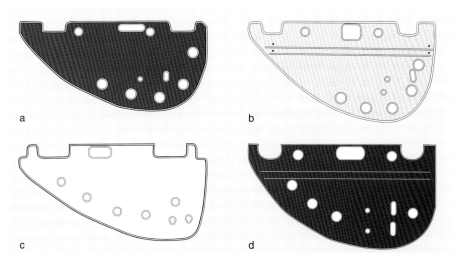

Figure 4.17 Variations in leading-edge and tail shapes result in four types of fins: *(a)* flatter leading edge with rounded back, *(b)* rounded-radius leading edge with rounded back, *(c)* flatter leading edge with straight back, and *(d)* rounded-radius leading edge with straight back.

Rounded-radius, leading-edge fins—These fins drive the front of the ski into the water. Skis with these fins start the turn sooner and finish with more ski in the water.

Square or straight tail fins—These fins allow the skier the push harder on the ski during the on side, but require more effort on the off side to finish the turn.

Rounded-back fins—These fins have more tail slide on the off side, but maybe too much slide on the on side.

I have found that skiers tend to ski fin shapes as much as they do skis. Try several shapes until you find one that fits your style. Once you settle on a shape, think about fine-tuning the fin with these three adjustments (see figure 4.18):

Horizontal adjustment—Moving the fin forward in the direction of the ski tip and backward toward the tail controls the front of the ski on the on-side turn. A forward adjustment will lift the front of the ski and drop the tail. A backward adjustment will drive the front of the ski into the water.

Vertical adjustment—Moving the fin up toward the top of the ski and down in the direction of the ski bottom controls turning stability, ease, and holding power for both on- and off-side turns. Moving the fin up makes the ski easier to turn and increases tail slide. A downward adjustment increases stability and reduces tail slide yet makes it harder to turn.

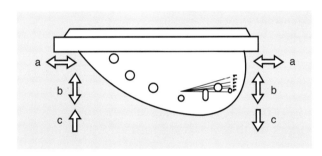

Figure 4.18 **You can fine-tune your fin with** *(a)* **horizontal adjustment,** *(b)* **vertical adjustment, and** *(c)* **diagonal adjustment.**

Diagonal adjustment—A diagonal adjustment either increases or decreases the leading edge length and controls the off-side turn. A longer, fuller leading edge drives the front of the ski into the water making for a quicker, more aggressive turn. A shorter leading edge raises the front of the ski resulting in a longer, rounded turn.

Troubleshooting Your Fin Adjustment

Problem: You break at the waist during off-side turns.

Solution: Make a diagonal adjustment by moving the front of the fin up into the ski.

Problem: Your ski will not initiate turns on both on and off sides.

Solution: Make a horizontal adjustment by moving the entire fin forward toward the front of the ski, or make a vertical adjustment by moving the entire fin up into the ski.

Problem: The ski tip rides high or out of the water in on-side turns.

Solution: Make a horizontal adjustment by moving the entire fin backward toward the tail of the ski.

Problem: The ski tip bites, or is too much in the water, during on-side turns.

Solution: Make a horizontal adjustment by moving the entire fin forward toward the front of the ski.

Problem: Edge change is too slow; the ski makes long, slow downcourse turns. The front of the ski comes out of the water at the end of the turn on either side.

Solution: Make a vertical adjustment by moving the entire fin up into the ski reducing the fin depth, or a horizontal adjustment by moving the entire fin forward toward the front of the ski.

Problem: The ski is too responsive or edgy. The tail of the ski slides around in the turn. The tail washes out or blows out at the end of the turn.

Solution: Make a vertical adjustment by moving the entire fin down out of the ski increasing the fin depth, or a horizontal adjustment by moving the entire fin backward toward the tail of the ski.

Wing Adjustments   Ski tuning is not complete without understanding the effects of the wing. Wing size and shape affect ski performance, but the primary purpose of the wing is to aid in slowing the ski down before the turn and to stabilize the ski in the preturn.

Higher on the ski—When the wing is closer to the bottom of the ski, you will experience more deceleration, and breaking. The ski also rolls up on edge more as a result in an increase in tip pressure on the on-side turn.

Lower on the ski—When the wing is farther from the bottom of the ski, you will experience more stability through the wakes and in the turns. The ski will turn better on the off-side turn as a result of the increase in tip pressure.

Increased wing angle—Increasing the wing angle increases drag and slows the ski down more quickly.

Decreased wing angle—Decreasing the wing angle allows you to carry more speed through the turn.

The combinations of ski settings are endless. Remember that making passes is what matters most. You could spend the rest of your life searching for that elusive perfect setting. Be careful not to fall into the tuning trap. So many variables adjust and are altered from one set to another that it is easy to lose site of the fundamentals of good slalom skiing. Adjust only one thing at a time, and track your performances and settings. Find a setting that is consistent and feels comfortable, and then spend your time working on the fundamentals of good body position and gate shots.

Chapter 5

Wakeboarding

Recently, I was reminded why I love wakeboarding. After arriving home from a week out of town for work, I took my four kids (ages 10, 6 , 5, and 2) out the next morning for a few hours on the lake. Their current on-water passion is wakeboarding. They learn new moves every time they hit the water, and seeing the pure excitement on their faces is priceless. The ease of learning wakeboarding is an important feature of the sport for kids or beginners of any age. People enjoy the feeling of accomplishment they get each time they go out on the wakeboard. Each time, they can get better.

My day with my kids didn't end with them practicing their moves; it got even better. After seeing the true novices of the sport in action in the morning, we headed to a professional contest being held not far from our home. "Awe inspiring" best describes seeing these men and women launch themselves into the air; contort their bodies into insane angles, positions, and twists; and land as though they were sitting down into a chair. Although learning and gaining some proficiency in wakeboarding may be relatively easy, by no means are the gnarly moves of the top boarders easy to perform. Incredible agility, balance, and guts are required to even attempt some of the moves. Seeing such a tremendous spectrum of ability in one day reinforced the importance of developing a smart, consistent method for learning from the start.

Body Position and Movements

The basic body position for wakeboarding is similar to that for snowboarding, surfing, and to a certain extent, skateboarding. Strive to maintain a low center of gravity. You should be aligned in an athletic stance over the board in dynamic balance relative to the pull of the boat. You must stand to counter the force of the boat just as a snowboarder stands in relation to the angle of the hill or a surfer stands in relation to the size of the wave. This alignment and stance are needed for stability and quick weight shifts or board tipping to change direction.

Because the feet are perpendicular to the direction of the board and boat, tipping movements (to control edge gripping and direction) are made using the heel and toes, similar to snowboarding. Flexing and extending the legs should happen as part of the natural timing of turning the board, approaching the wake, and landing. Tipping keeps you aligned so you can maintain edge control. Counteracting movements, which are more difficult, are used for advanced moves in which rotation is needed. The counteracting movements help stack the body into a solid, aligned position so rotation occurs on an axis. The fore–aft balance on a wakeboard is maintained relative to the rope or pull from the boat and is controlled by the location of the hips relative to the feet and the pressure put on the arch of the foot.

Learning Progression

The learning progression for wakeboarding builds on a few basic skills and movements. Learning to execute those movements properly will allow you to learn more advanced tricks faster with fewer falls and more fun. You will see in the trick descriptions how each trick builds on or originates from others. For example, an S-bend starts off with the basic skill of progressive edging. Aligning and positioning your progressive edge gives you the counterrotation needed for loading the rope and getting the air required to elevate yourself with control, balance, and enough force to extend and rotate and perform the rest of the trick.

This section focuses on perfecting the skills you will need to learn the full repertoire of tricks possible on a wakeboard. Once you get the feeling of how to tip the board and progressively edge up the wake, you will open up every other trick in the book.

Following are seven classifications of tricks that riders perform on the water:

- **Surface tricks** are those performed while the rider is not in the air but rather riding across the water; they are the side slide, wake surf, and bunny hop.
- **Grabs** are the various ways a rider can grab the board while in the air.
- **Spins** are tricks in which the rider rotates the board and body in the air. These include the 360 and 540.
- **Inverts** are when the rider goes upside down; these tricks (also called flipping) include the front flip, half cab, backflip, roll-to-revert, and scarecrow.
- **Tantrum tricks,** such as the tantrum and whirlybird, are performed leading with the back. The board follows and the rider stops tipping or edging as he approaches the wake.
- **Raley-based tricks** are based on the air raley, in which the board goes above the rider's head; these include the hoochie glide and S-bend.
- **Handle pass inverts,** such as a mobius, are tricks in which the rider combines an invert and a spin requiring a handle pass

Getting Up

To perform any trick on a wakeboard, you first need to learn how to get up out of the water. Before you try to get up, shorten the rope to 30 to 50 feet (9 to 15 m). This provides a direct pull. When the rope is connected to a tower, it actually lifts you up rather than dragging you across the water. With your body facing the boat, and the board perpendicular to the boat, do the following:

1. Pull your ankles in close to your bottom with your knees close to your chest in a squatting position. The closer you are to the board, the easier the start will be.
2. Keep your arms extended and placed on each side of your knees. Hold the handle with your palms facing down.
3. Push your chest slightly up. Make sure the toe of the board is slightly above water.

Now you're ready for the fun part. A slow and gradual speed increase is all you need to pull you out of the water (see figure 5.1), but you'll need a driver with a smooth hand. The maximum speed should be around 14 to 18 miles per hour (23 to 29 km/h). Relax and hold your position, allowing the board to naturally

Figure 5.1 **When learning to get up on a wakeboard, relax and let the boat and board do the work.**

swing toward the boat as you plane out of the water. Stay in an athletic, dynamic, balanced position with as little tension as possible on the rope and in your legs.

Wake Crossing

Once you have established balance, begin trying to tip the board heel side first and then toe side, as shown in figure 5.2, until you feel edge control and begin to understand how to maintain balance in relation to the rope and boat. Once you get the feeling of how to move the board within the wakes, try crossing the wakes first on the heel side and then back across on the toe side. Do this with a slight heel-side tip of the board away from the boat. Now do the same thing on the toe side of the board. Tip the board by pressing on your toes. As you ride over the wake, you will feel it push you up, causing your knees to bend or compress into your body. If you have some speed, you may feel a bit of air under the board as you come down the wake.

Figure 5.2 **Maintaining balance on the board requires learning to tip the *(a)* heel side of the board and the *(b)* toe side of the board.**

Hip position is also essential for crossing wakes. Focus on rotating your hips so that your chest is facing the boat and your hips, knees, and ankles are in alignment with the rope. To turn the board in either direction, tip the board on edge with a move of the hips in the direction you want to cross the wake (e.g., turning your hips to the left causes your body to turn the board left). The move is the same whether you are crossing one wake or two: use your hips to tip the edge of the board.

Once you have mastered basic wake crossing, you can surf the wake (see figure 5.3) to tip and edge the board with varying degrees of aggressiveness and intensity. Edge up and down the wake as if you were trying to make a big spray. Feel how the more you tip the board, the more edge control, or grip, you have and the more pressure you feel on the handle. This force also compresses your legs as you approach the wake. Begin with long, smooth turns and edges, or tipping movements, and build up to shorter and harder moves.

Figure 5.3   **Wake surfing teaches how to control heel-side and toe-side board tipping.**

Edging Through the Wake

If you are a surfer, then you know about waves. A wake is similar to a wave in the ocean. Surfers need to understand the dynamics of the ocean, tides, and winds to know how waves are created and when and where to surf. Similarly, wakeboarders need to understand the dynamics of a wake to get air. As a boat travels across a flat lake, it displaces water, which creates a wake. The heavier the boat, the bigger the wake because more energy is pushing the water. As a result, there is more force, or energy, to propel you higher. You want to use the energy of the wake to push you up into the air rather than try to jump off the top of the wake. By learning this skill correctly, you use less energy on the takeoff and have more control and strength for more complex moves once you are in the air.

Getting "big air" begins by learning how to create energy as you approach the wake. Progressive tipping for edging is the most important skill for every wakeboarder to master. Start by gradually edging, or tipping, the board first on the heel side (see figure 5.4). Edging the board into and up the wake creates the energy needed for pushing against the force of the wake. As you hit the wake, you release that energy by simply extending your knees, thus pushing the board against the energy of the wake. The key is to increase your edge pressure, or tip angle, as you get closer to the top of the wake. When done correctly, you get pushed into the air proportional to the energy you create with your edge up the wake. Creating the correct body position, alignment, and stacking against the boat as you approach the wake both heel side and toe side takes time to master and is a skill that you should work on consistently.

The following steps break edging down move by move:

1. Edge out beside the boat 10 to 15 feet (3 to 4.6 m) and make a slow, smooth tip of the board, letting the board move under the rope until you feel the boat start to pull you back toward the wake.

2. Maintain the tipped edge of the board as you approach the wake, and gently increase the tip edge. You will pick up speed as you tip the edge of the board. Think about continuously turning the board in an arc toward the wake while showing more of the base of your board to the boat.

3. Continue to build up your edge tipping and increase your knee flexion and counterrotation away from the boat to the top of the wake. You will feel an increased pull in your hands as you climb the wake. Be sure to keep the handle down at your waist. Many riders mistakenly think that to get height, they must edge as hard as they can, as long as they can, and generate speed into the wake. There is no doubt that a hard, fast edge, or tip, will develop a lot of speed and give you distance, but it won't give you any height. Such an approach uses too much force early in the arc toward the wake and does not generate lift from the wake.

Figure 5.4 Learning how to build and control a progressive edge is essential for getting air off the wake.

4. As you ride up the wake on edge, extend your knees! Stay in dynamic balance in relation to the slope of the wake and the pull of the rope, typically slightly away from the boat. Keep the handle by your waist, and move your hips toward the handle. Extend your chest and head up. In this position you can resist the force of the wake pushing up on you by pushing down against it. Imagine that you are trying to break the board in half at the crest of the wake.

5. The release of the energy you created with a proper tipping edge into the wake and your leg extension will result in what most describe as a pop or lift off the wake, similar to a double bounce on a trampoline as the wake's force reacts to your downward energy.

6. Keep your eyes open to spot the landing, and then absorb it with your knees and ankles to quickly establish edge control and continue out on edge away from the boat.

A common error when trying a progressive edge tip is to stop tipping the board or to flatten out. If you stop tipping the board at the wake, you reduce the energy stored in the board. The result is that the force created by edging at the wake is lost. Always focus on driving your energy down against the wake so that the wake pushes you up with more force and you get more air.

Learning Order for Tricks

The learning order presented here for wakeboard tricks follows a skill development pattern and builds from one trick to the next. Though you may be tempted to try launching yourself into an air raley right from the beginning, a smarter approach is to learn the tricks in (or fairly close to) the order below. Doing so will keep help keep you safe, eliminate frustration, and make you a stronger, more consistent rider.

There are four features concerning the development and transfer of skills as you learn new moves on the water.

1. Focus on doing whatever it takes to ride out the trick. A focus on the outcome will allow individual variability and style in the trick but keep the general principles of the technique intact.

2. There is more skill transfer from the relatively difficult (complex) tricks to the relatively easy (simple) tricks rather than the other way round. So sometimes it works best to use the moves you can make to determine what to learn next rather than what is perceived to be the easiest by others.

3. The greatest difficulties in transfer skills usually have to do with time and directional relations. Because of this, it is vital to always teach and learn the reverse as well as the basic move and prepare learners at an early stage for this variability.

4. Age matters. Efficient learning of new skills and moves are largely functions of aging. Thus the methods which are best for young people may not be best for people who are well into adulthood.

Side Slide

The side slide is technically turning the board 90 degrees on the surface. It is a great trick to help you learn balance as well as how the subtle movements of your feet control the tipping of the board and the grip of the edges. It will also help you learn to counterbalance against the rope and board to remain in a balanced body position. A side slide can be done either outside or inside the wake. To perform a side slide, put more weight on your heels and tip the back edge into the water. You will know you are doing it right when some spray comes out from under your board. Now try the same move on the toe side. This side is a bit more difficult and may take some extra time to learn. Both side slides really build great tipping and counterbalancing skills, as well as a feel for how to control the board.

Lip Slide

A lip slide is a side slide done on the crest of the wake. This is a great practice drill for developing a feel for the counterbalance and body alignment needed for more advanced tricks. Begin by positioning yourself on the crest of the wake. Do a side slide with a slight heel-side tip of the board and a forward push of your back foot while the board tracks the very top of the wake.

Surface 180

Once you can tip and control the edges of your board, you are ready for the 180. If you are riding your board with your left foot forward, you will rotate to the left. If you are riding with your right foot forward, you will rotate to the right. Try to place your weight over the center of the board. In one smooth motion, swing the board around leading with your rear foot. Once you are in the 180 position, place more weight on the tip to allow the board to track for stability. To get back around to the starting position, do the opposite move by swinging the rear foot back behind the front foot.

Surface 360

The surface 360 is next in the progression and is as simple as doing a surface 180, holding that position for a moment, and then continuing the rotation around to the front. Again, if you're riding with your left foot forward, you will rotate left. If you're riding with your right foot forward, you will rotate to the right. To turn in either direction, pull the handle in toward you and turn in the same motion. Let go with your trailing hand and bend the elbow of the hand holding the handle around the small of your lower back to make the handle pass. Reach with your free hand and grab the handle and pull yourself until you've made it to the front position. A smooth, continuous pull on the rope combined with controlled balance will make this an easy trick to learn. Focus on pulling in the rope and advancing on the boat to give you time to make the full rotation.

Ollie (Bunny Hop)

Pushing the board down into the water will cause the water to push back. This energy provides the air needed for executing an ollie. Think of jumping on a trampoline: you push down, and the energy stored in the springs is released to push you up. Starting in a neutral stance, in one move drop your body by flexing your ankles and knees and push the board into the water with a quick, forceful extension of your legs, standing tall as you get pushed up out of the water. The more energy you have in your push, the higher you go.

You can also do an ollie 180, which combines an ollie with a 180-degree change in direction outside the wake by hopping into the air. Once you get the ollie down, initiate a rotation with your hips and knees to move the board once it breaks the surface of the water. Similar to the regular ollie, push down with your rear foot on the tail of the board. When you get enough air to free the rear fin, rotate around with a counterrotation of the shoulders and a twist of the hips in the direction of the turn until your opposite foot is toward the boat (also known as riding fakie or switch stance).

Air (One Wake)

This is a key move to master because it will lead you to more advanced air and wake tricks. It is the first trick in which you use the skill of edging through the wake. Mastering this skill is critical to your jumping as you improve and begin to crave more air. You need to learn the correct way to jump over one wake and land on edge or with the board tipped away from the boat. Approach the wake with a moderate edge, or tip, of the board. As you go up the wake, keep your knees slightly flexed and extend your legs with a push through both feet to get some air. Keep the board on edge until you are ready to land.

Backside Air (Two Wakes)

In the backside air you jump across two wakes from the heel side. Getting enough air to cross both wakes and land out past the wakes (referred to as "in the flats") depends on your skill in edging through the wake. Your maximum tip and edge must be at the top of the wake. Make a gradual turn and set your edge as you build angle and speed toward the wake and flex your legs. Extend your legs when you reach the top of the wake and hold on until you cross the second wake.

Frontside Air (Two Wakes)

As in the backside air over two wakes, with the frontside (or toe-side) air, you must clear both wakes. It all starts with the ever-important edge up and through the wake. As you approach the top of the wake, focus on keeping tension in the handle and leaning your body into the tip of the board to get your full force into the board. Try shortening the rope to about 40 feet (12 m) to get the feel of this move and let it out a few feet (or about a meter) at a time as you learn the toe-side tipping and counterbalance needed for controlling the board on the toe side.

Air 180 (Two Wakes)

To perform the air 180, you use the wake to get air and change directions, clearing two wakes. An air 180 initially seems easier to do frontside than backside. Starting this trick from the toe side allows you to rotate toward the boat and land facing the same direction. With a heel-side approach, your rotation isn't too difficult, but the landing is almost with your back to the boat. On this side, focus on keeping the rope near your hip and bend your knees to maintain the direction of the board.

360 Heli (Two Wakes)

For the 360 heli, you use the wake to get into the air and rotate the board 360 degrees. Start with a slight counterrotation of your hips and lead the rotation with your head and let the rest of your body follow. Keep your position vertical to slightly back to remain on axis as the boat pulls you forward.

Backside Air With Grab (Two Wakes)

Here's a trick to get you comfortable grabbing the board. Basic wakeboard grabs involve various combinations of front and back hands grabbing front and back sides of the board. For the backside air with grab, you do a heel-side air with any grab on the board with either hand. Establish a strong edge into the wake to clear both wakes, and grab the board in whatever way you feel comfortable while in the air. The only thing you want to think about is bringing the board up to you by pulling your knees into your chest rather than reaching down to the board or bending at your waist.

Back Scratcher

The back scratcher is a move in which you kick the board up behind your back. Set a solid tip and edge to get lift. As you approach the top of your lift, bend your knees to a 90-degree angle, bringing your feet and the board behind you and away from the boat.

After you have learned the back scratcher, you can try the method, which is a back scratcher with a heel-side grab. As with the back scratcher, bend your knees to a 90-degree angle so the board reaches back toward your rear. Then, with your leading hand, reach back and grab the top of the middle part of the board.

Stiffy

The stiffy requires that you extend (or bone out) both legs in front of you. The stiffy is pretty much the opposite of a back scratcher. As you go off the wake, straighten out your legs and bring the board completely forward. Imagine that you are showing the bottom of the board to everyone in the boat.

Grab 180

For the grab 180, you get into the air, complete a grab, and land facing the opposite direction you were facing at takeoff. Combining a 180 and a grab can often be tricky. Remember to pull the board up to you to make the grab. It may take some trial and error, so get comfortable grabbing any part of the board with either hand. As you get better, you can try the more complicated combinations.

Roast Beef

The roast beef is a rear-hand heel-side grab that you make between the feet and through the legs. This trick shouldn't be a hard one to learn. If you're getting good air and landing pretty consistently, you can begin doing board grab tricks starting with the roast beef. As you jump the wake, bring your knees to your chest, reach through your legs with your trailing hand, and grab the middle of the board.

Indy Stiffy

The indy stiffy is like a regular stiffy in which you straighten out your legs and bring the board completely forward. The difference is that once the board is out in front of you, you reach out and grab the top of the middle of the board with your back hand.

Slob Heli

The slob heli combines a toe-side grab with a 360-degree rotation over one or two wakes. Approach the wake as you would for a normal heli, but use a slightly more aggressive board tip and counter to get higher in the air so you can make the grab. Make the grab as you begin your rotation with your front hand on the front toe-side edge of your board (known as a slob grab). Once you complete the rotation, release the grab with your front hand, quickly make the handle pass at the small of your back, and then stick the landing as you would for a normal 360. The key to this trick is getting enough height to make a solid grab.

Backside Back Roll

This trick provides the first invert trick in the learning order. From 15 feet (4.6 m) outside the wake, take a heel-side tip into the wake. The key to the roll is to load the line by tipping the board all the way through the wake and making a strong countering move away from the boat and into the wake. The invert or roll is initiated by the countering move and the load of the rope. Maintain a balanced body position, turn your head over your right shoulder for a right-foot-forward approach, and keep advancing the board away from the boat. Keep the handle down low to generate rotation.

Backside Roll-to-Revert

The backside roll-to-revert is similar to the backside back roll except that you land riding fakie. The first half of the backside roll-to-revert is exactly like the backside back roll. The difference is that you must commit more to being backward as you approach the wake by almost cheating, or prerotating the board around, as you approach the wake. Once you hit the peak of your lift, let go with your hand that is farther from the boat and spot your landing. Letting go of the handle will automatically rotate you and your board to the fakie position.

Half Cab

The half cab is a switch-stance back roll. You perform it as you would a back roll, but you just need to be strong coming into the wake from the opposite direction. Approach from 15 feet (4.6 m) with a smooth tip. As you leave the wake, make the board slide away from the boat as you keep your core strong and the handle down low. Drop your outside shoulder, and let go with your front hand.

Frontside Back Roll

The approach for the frontside back roll starts about 15 to 20 feet (4.6 to 6 m) outside of the wake on your toe side with an aggressive progressive tip of the board into the wake. Stay aligned with an erect posture balanced over your toes as you come up the wake. Hold that tipped edge and keep even pressure on the balls of your feet as your board reaches the top of the wake. This will keep the nose of the board heading up and away from the boat. Now simply look back over your right shoulder if you ride left foot forward. It helps to let go with the hand farther from the boat as you begin the roll.

Tantrum

The tantrum is a backflip done with the body first in the direction of the takeoff. In diving terms, this trick is like doing a gainer off the wake. Approach the wake with a strong heel-side board tip. As you start to come up the wake, shift to your toe-side edge, square your shoulders to the wake, and throw your head back and over the top of the wake like a high jumper clearing the bar. Let the board lead your head, and let the wake kick you around. The transition to the toe-side edge is the key.

Backside Air Raley

Starting heel side, go into the air and raise the board above your body (pushing the board up so it is inverted). Begin by pulling out wide on your backside edge, make a smooth progressive tip of the board, and set a hard edge. Maintain the edge through the wake and out away from the boat.

When you are learning the backside air raley, at first just jump over the wakes and learn to control the board tip and edge. As you begin to take a more aggressive edge, let the handle out away from your body and let the board travel from under you. Move the board out in small increments until you can fully extend it above your head. You should feel a stretch of your abdominal muscles as the board travels out from under you. The landing is initiated with a contraction of your abdominal muscles to pull the board back under you as you push the handle straight down and to your waist. Pulling in will not help; you need to push the handle down.

Combination Moves

With a solid foundation of moves locked down, you are now ready for some advanced combination moves. When you reach this level, you should consider finding a good coach to help you. At this level, you will also need to know how to double-up for big air. A double-up on a wakeboard is using the energy from two wakes to get even bigger air. There are three things to think about when learning to do a double-up. First, you need a driver who understands how to create the double-up wake. Next, you need to know what wake to hit. You will see three rollers of progressive size. The second roller is the most frequently hit. The third is larger and steeper, but you will have more difficulty getting a clean approach to it. The last thing you need to think about is the most important—the timing. You need to time your approach so that the roller and wake come together to make a V as you ride up. If you arrive too early or too late, you won't get the lift and the wake will push back on you.

Scarecrow

The scarecrow is a toe-side front roll-to-revert. It starts with an aggressive toe-side board tip 15 feet (4.6 m) out from the wake and moves into a front roll. As you leave the wake, tuck your chin and head and look under your back armpit to initiate the rotation. At the top of the front roll you do a 180 twist to land in a switch-stance position. Focus on keeping your hips moving away up the wake and rotating your shoulders away from the boat to initiate the 180 twist at the top of the roll.

Backside Mobius

The backside mobius is a heel-side rotational roll and combination flip with a handle pass. Start out only about 10 feet (3 m) outside the wake to make sure you maintain balance and control as you tip the board and edge away from the boat and up the wake. Imagine that you are doing a roll-to-revert and move your head and shoulders back. As you rotate to fakie, take your back hand and put it into the small of your back and reach for the handle. Once you get the handle, it will rotate you the rest of the way.

S-Bend

The S-bend is a backside air raley with a 360 body rotation while the board is extended. Start out wide outside the wake and take a super-aggressive board tip into the wake as if you were doing a raley. As you leave the wake, put your head between your arms and rotate inward, driving your board above your head. As you finish rotating 360 degrees overhead, look to spot your landing.

Chapter 6

Trick Skiing

The most dedicated and determined athletes on the water are trick skiers. Hall of fame trickers Britt and Tawn Larsen one year skied 100 days in a row. That is the type of dedication and determination it takes to be a world record holder and world champion. Becoming truly successful at trick skiing takes a great deal of practice. Tricking champion Jimmy Siemers always says that he put his time in at an early age. Considering that he started skiing as a small child, that early start has added up to lots and lots of time, and it shows.

The trick event is the ultimate test of the four fundamental skills (edge control, pressure control, rotation, and balance) and a great way to practice the tipping, flexing, extending, counterrotation, as well as counterbalance and fore–aft balance, movements critical to all on-water events. This is not meant to intimidate you or scare you away from this awe-inspiring event; rather, it is a statement of respect for the time and effort it takes to become a good tricker.

The good news is that although trick skiing is an athletic challenge, it also is the easiest event to get into and enjoy. Early on, the learning progresses quickly and is fun, with new tricks being learned almost daily. Tricking offers an advantage over slalom and jumping because courses and jumps are not required; all you need is some water. The water conditions are less critical, because you trick ski at much slower speeds. This can also save money on gas because you will not need a powerful boat. I learned to trick behind a 35-horsepower aluminum skiff, and we could trick all day on a 6-gallon (23 L) tank. The slow speed also makes these events less painful, which is a good thing because falling is part of learning to trick.

You will improve in your other event skills by learning how to ride trick skis. As mentioned, performing tricks forces you to develop excellent balance, strong pressure and edge control, and smooth turning skills. The awareness you acquire of your body in space and how to control the forces of the boat, rope, and water makes you a better skier overall. Another benefit of tricking is that tricks offer a great change of pace and won't wear out your hands and body the way slalom, jumping, and wakeboarding will.

The introduction of lighter carbon fiber trick skis and the near-universal acceptance of hard-shell bindings in younger trickers have opened up the event and changed the way tricks are taught. The influence of wakeboarding and boats with towers have also changed trickers' motivation to go for big air tricks. The better tipping edge control offered by hard-shell bindings is an important part of this equation as well, allowing better feathering of pressure control so skiers can load the rope and learn the big air tricks more easily. The consistency of boat speed provided by speed control systems has also had a positive impact on trick training and learning.

Body Position and Basic Skills

Rising out of the water on two trick skis is the same as on two regular skis. Things can get a bit slippery once you are up, however, because trick skis have no fins to stabilize them. This makes learning tipping for edge control movements essential to riding trick skis. At first they are more difficult to control, and you may need a few tries before you get into a comfortable and stable position. The key is to focus on balance. Everyone learning to trick takes the same goofy falls, and they all are related to balance. Minimize pulling in on the rope or standing up quickly. Take your time and develop patience; you will need it to become an accomplished tricker. You must first learn, feel, and understand correct body position and control of trick skis. Once you have that down, you will be ready to learn the basic tricks and skills.

Chapter 4 noted the value of dry land practice for slalom skiing. For trick skiing, dry land practice is even more essential to your success. You must really see and feel on dry land the movements you need to make on the water. Practicing on dry land provides opportunities to discuss and correct your movements. If you have a coach, you can get immediate hands-on attention and feedback. Learning inclination and angulation is far easier on land than on the water. Save yourself and your boat crew time and frustration by learning every trick on land before taking it to the water.

To get a good simulation on dry land of the pull from the boat, set up a simple pulley system on the dock or at home. At the very least, tie a handle to a tree to practice the various movements each trick requires. The time you spend getting the feeling of these movements has two benefits: (1) it enables you to work on various tricks or simulate runs, and (2) it gives you the chance to build strength and muscles. It's not about how much weight you can move; it's about practicing lots and lots of pulls until your muscles fatigue. The dry land practice will also spare you numerous falls on the water, and you'll save fuel.

The first thing to practice on land is body position. A mirror can be helpful for checking your position. The correct body position for two- and one-ski trick skiing includes knees and ankles bent, back straight, handle held with both palms down at waist height, and head and eyes facing the horizon (see figure 6.1). You can't tell in the photos, but the skier's weight is centered over the skis. Imitate this position on land and get it right. Now let's take it to the water.

Figure 6.1   **Stable body position for *(a)* two-ski and *(b)* one-ski trick skiing.**

As noted, trick skis feel slippery at first. So, in addition to learning a dynamically balanced body position, you need to learn how to tip the skis to get the grip, or edge control, to stabilize the skis. Keep your speed slow to help improve the grip of the edges in the water—about 11 to 15 mph (18 to 24 km/h) for a 150-pound (68 kg) adult. Why is slower better than faster? The faster the boat speed is, the harder the water's surface is and the more difficult it is to tip the skis onto their edges. Practice and become comfortable with two trick skis before trying any tricks.

Skill 1: Progressive Tipping or Edging

The first skill is to learn how to tip the skis on edge, ride up the wake, and pop or jump off the wake. (This is similar to the same skill performed on a wakeboard. Refer to chapter 5 for information about the dynamics of a wake.) Begin with a small tipping movement to change direction when you are between the wakes. Then widen and lengthen the movements until you are able to cross both wakes. Now try extending your legs and pushing through your feet to pop off the wake. Continue to get more aggressive and progressive with your tipping. Eventually, try jumping over both wakes as you continue to edge from side to side like a slalom skier. This movement teaches you to tip and ride the edge of your skis in motion across the path of the boat.

To tip and edge quickly and aggressively, you need to understand angulation; that is, the angle you need at various joints in your lower body—primarily your hips. Figure 6.2 shows a skier tipping and edging with angulation. Notice the low position and flex of the ankles and knees as they assist in helping to edge the skis as the hips move laterally toward the direction of the wake. Angulation moves the hips radically to the inside of the turn or in most cases laterally toward the boat. Trickers who have mastered angulation can do advanced moves on the crest of a wake and never move their upper body off the crest of the wake, slide down the wake, or lose their balance. They move their skis, however, 2 to 3 feet (60 to 90 cm) from side to side to get air.

To feel the movement of angulation, sit about halfway back on a chair with both feet together on the floor and your knees together. If you move your knees apart, your hip joints rotate in the sockets. Keeping your knees apart, slide your feet apart and point your toes outward. Again, this movement creates rotation in the hips. Your knees stay over your feet and in line with your thighs. Now, roll one of your ankles to the little-toe side of your foot, and you will see the leg move, or rotate, farther out. When you roll the ankle to the big-toe side of your foot, your knee, thigh, and hip move inward as well. Although the knee and ankle move, rotation in the hip joint is what makes the movement possible. The ankle and knee mostly flex forward or extend.

Skill 2: Handle Control (Advancing and Dragging)

Getting the feeling of advancing on the boat by properly controlling the handle is a critical skill. Think of handle control as the free throw of tricking. All trickers, no matter what their skill level, must practice this constantly. To perform tricks, you must understand how to break free from the forward pull of the boat by advancing on the boat or rope. In other words, you must move toward the boat faster than the boat is pulling you.

Figure 6.2 **Angulation is a movement to master if you want to improve your trick skiing.**

You accomplish handle control by using a progressively stronger pull on the rope. The strongest pull should be at the end of the inward pull. To try this skill at first, you can start with just a pull on the rope or you can even jerk the rope in to your waist as shown in figure 6.3. When you do this, you will see the skis advance toward the boat. Continue this technique and try to maintain a balanced stance with good body position. Over time, make this a smooth, controlled pull. Practice it with one hand and then the other, and then with both hands. Advancing on the rope is an essential skill for most flips, body-over tricks, and toe tricks in which everything depends on having the rope assist you. This skill also allows you to use the rope as an aid in rotating around your axis. Handle control is extremely important in tricking, so take your time and get these relatively simple skills down.

In addition to advancing on the boat, you need to be able to slow yourself down using drag, or friction, to establish control of your skis. Leaning backward or putting more pressure on the tail of the ski creates drag and slows you down. Between advancing and drag is just gliding on the surface, remaining relaxed with minimum friction, which may feel very slippery at first. For this reason, your stance on the ski is essential. Applying too much pressure on the tail or leaning back too far creates drag, or friction, as does leaning too far forward. Balancing on the whole foot creates the least amount of friction, and this along with advancing using the rope makes gliding possible. Handle control requires an understanding of how to advance, how to create and use gliding, and how to create friction. This understanding will help you learn new tricks or perform the ones you know more consistently.

To understand handle control, try just standing in the front stance in the middle of the wakes. Bend forward at the waist and let your arms extend out in front. In this position try to even turn the ski to the back. It's almost impossible. This illustrates the importance of having the rope handle close to your waist as you pivot the ski tip to the back.

Figure 6.3 Pulling the rope into your waist is a way to begin learning handle control so that you can learn to advance on the boat.

Tricking Drills and Games

This section discusses a few ways to maximize your time and skill improvement. Inclement weather during the season and cold weather in the off-season may limit your on-water time, but it does not need to stop you from improving, learning, and developing your skills.

- **Tricking on ice.** Using a trick ski or skis, have someone pull you slowly across the ice. Once friction is broken, the skis will move effortlessly. At this point you may realize that the only way to do surface tricks is to learn how to control the rope. If you pull too hard, you will lose your balance; if you pull too softly, you will not have enough energy to rotate completely. You can also use this method to learn toe tricks. Practicing on ice will help you learn how to regulate rope control and will demonstrate how keeping your body skeletally aligned gives you dynamic balance while moving. The skills you learn in this drill will transfer back to the water.

- **Wake-to-wake jumping.** Besides learning to edge, you should learn to jump one wake or both wakes on your trick skis. To jump both wakes, you need to tip the edge to load the skis so that they can pop, or jump, up into the air. As in wakeboarding, without edging, getting the skis to lift off the water is difficult. You need a platform or solid base under your feet or they will slip out from under you, just like they do when you try to jump up from a running start on an icy pond. Edging so you can pressure and load the skis is important. After you master jumping both wakes, you can go one step further by jumping over both wakes in both directions. Then jump and see how high you can get up off the water as you clear both wakes, and see if you can jump two feet outside the bottom of the second wake. If you are unable to edge after landing, tip the skis, or you will be unstable and end up spending time in the water rather than on top of it. Jumping both wakes isn't about getting air; it's about learning to tip for edge control so you can load the skis and push up as if you were on a trampoline.

- **Handle pass.** Learning to pass the handle takes a lot of time, but you have no hope of being a successful tricker if you miss the handle. A great place to practice the handle pass is on dry land so you don't waste time on the water. The best time to practice this drill is during the preseason. Have someone hold the rope and stand or sit about 5 to 10 feet (1.5 to 3 m) away. This person should help take up the slack in the rope and regulate the rope's tension so that it mimics actually skiing on the water. If another person is not available, you can practice with a rope attached to a stationary object, but this method is less effective. As you practice passing the handle, focus on learning to keep your axis stable as you rotate.

- **Battle.** This drill is a great way to learn and improve balance. Two people get on their trick skis at the same rope length and ski side by side. Each skier can edge, spray, and push the other skier. The goal is for each skier to stay upright while making the other skier fall over. Both skiers should exercise caution and good sense. They should not do dangerous moves such as jumping into or on top of each other.

Learning Progressions

The learning progressions for trick skiing will help you gain strength, confidence, and skill as you learn each new trick. The progressions start with basic tricks to help you develop dynamic balance and ski tipping skills, and then progressively move to more advanced tricks that require more complicated combinations of movements. Make a conscious effort to focus and learn the movements for each trick first on land by doing several repetitions before taking it to the water. Look at the photos and imitate those position and movements. Start slow and really feel the muscles you are using. It doesn't matter if you can't perform the trick at the outset; you can still work on the movements. Water time is not all that counts. You need to learn to move and be fluid. The key is to make it fun.

Basic Tricks

To become an accomplished trick skier, you need to build a strength and skill foundation and build from it progressively. The tricks in this section are the building blocks that provide the fundamental moves you need. Many of the more advanced tricks are combinations of these moves.

Side Slide

This is the first trick you should learn. It teaches balance, control of the rope and handle, and the body position that underlies all tricks. The steps for performing this trick are as follows:

1. Establish a solid body position.
2. Make a firm, even pull on the rope into your waist.
3. Turn the skis 90 degrees with your knees, hips, and shoulders (see figure 6.4). It may help to let go with one hand and turn in the direction of your free hand.
4. Keep the handle at your waist and maintain an upright position during the turn.

Your knees must remain soft and flexible during the turn. Keep the skis spread slightly for stability and your free arm extended for balance. If the skis slip out during the turn, the cause is usually leaning away from the boat with the upper body. Correct this error by centering your weight over the skis, keeping a balanced stance, and bending your ankles. Remember to keep your weight on the whole foot or with slightly more weight on the balls of your feet.

Figure 6.4 **The side slide.**

Front to Back

The front to back (also known as the back) is the first trick that gets them cheering in the boat. The back is simply a continuation of the side slide, except that you complete the rotation to a 180-degree turn (see figure 6.5). You will get some looks from other boats when people see you cruising down the lake backward. It is easy to do this trick on a kneeboard if you have one, which will teach you the pull and rotation, as well as get you used to riding in the back position. Some have success doing this trick before the side slide. Do whatever feels more natural to you. Here are the steps for performing this trick:

1. Begin from your basic position.
2. Pull the rope in firmly and smoothly to the hip opposite the direction in which you are going to turn.
3. Begin the turn by completing the pull-in, release the hand farther from the boat, and lead the turn with your hips.
4. Keep the handle close to your waist and turn the skis backward.
5. Grab the handle with your free hand and press it into the small of your back just above your rear. Once you are skiing backward, maintain the body position of the forward stance position: knees bent, back straight, handle in to the waist, body leaning counter or away from the boat slightly, and head and eyes up.

Simply turning to the back is the trick, but being able to comfortably ride in the back position is also important. You need to be stable in the back position to learn other tricks that involve this stance. Try skiing in and out of both wakes in the back position to develop the strength and balance you need for other tricks.

Figure 6.5 **The front to back.**

Back to Front

Now that you are skiing backward, it's time to turn around again and see where you are going. The key to the back to front (also known as the front) is keeping the handle close to your body and learning to pull on the rope from the back position (figure 6.6). Here are the steps:

1. Begin from the backward position.
2. Let go with one hand and keep the handle close to your waist; do not extend your arm away from your body.
3. Pull your handle hand to your stomach.

Figure 6.6 **The back to front.**

4. Rotate forward, keeping your chest up as you turn to maintain your vertical axis.

5. Grab the handle with your free hand and complete the rotation.

Reverse Back and Front

Once you can do the front to back and the back to front, turning in the direction that is natural for you, don't waste time. Learn the tricks in the opposite direction. These tricks are known as reverses. If you aspire to be a good tricker, you can't avoid the reverse tricks; so begin now and get the feeling of turning the opposite way. These tricks are done exactly the same way, but they may take longer to learn because you are not as strong or confident turning to the other side. Don't think about it. You know how to do it; just go out there and land it your first try.

360, or O, Front to Front

The 360 is the first trick that demonstrates the benefits of following a learning progression when learning to trick ski. The key to the 360 is dividing it into two 180s: a front to back followed by a back to front, continuing in the same direction. That is how you learn all multiple rotation tricks—by breaking them down into their basic tricks. Here are the steps:

1. Begin by doing a front to back.

2. Stop and hold the position for a moment.

3. Then do a back to front in the same direction.

4. Continue performing the trick in this manner, but pause for a shorter time.

The pause is called a "hitch" by most skiers, and the trick is to minimize the length of time in the hitch until it becomes continuous without a hitch. A few pointers for the smooth execution of this trick follow:

○ Make a slightly stronger pull in on the rope than you do for a 180.

○ Make a smooth exchange of the handle and keep it close to your body.

○ Keep your knees soft and flexed, with your weight or stance centered on the whole ski.

○ Maintain good skeletal alignment in a ready, relaxed position throughout the trick to help keep your head up and your eyes focused just above the horizon.

○ Think about pivoting the skis, turn your body at the same speed as the skis, and make smooth, continuous movements.

○ Maintain a tall, balanced stance on the skis, advance on the boat as you pull the rope handle in appropriately, turn or pivot as a unit around your axis, and keep the skis as flat on the surface of the water as possible.

Troubleshooting Basic Tricks

Three common falls occur when learning basic tricks. Following are descriptions of the falls, the errors that cause them, and solutions.

Fall: Away from the boat as you turn

Error: Looking down and shifting the rotational axis away from the boat

Solution: Focus your eyes above the horizon at the tops of the trees. Keep your head and shoulders up by sticking your chest out. Your goal is to remain balanced. The sensation in the front position is to lean back slightly or against the pull of the boat. If you have not advanced to the point of being able to take some of the tension off the rope, you may exaggerate the lean, bending at the waist and looking down to compensate for the pull of the boat. This puts your balance on the tip of the skis (because you are facing backward). As you correct your stance, you will find it much easier to ski with less drag.

Fall: Toward the boat in a backward position

Error: Ankles and knees are too stiff.

Solution: Stress the knee and ankle bend. Shift your weight to your toes as you turn, and maintain your position so that your knees and ankles are flexed. This provides more pressure on the balls of your feet than on your heels.

Fall: Forward when only halfway through the turn

Error: Not advancing on the boat enough or allowing the handle to leave your waist during the turn, resulting in the rope pulling you over; bending over so that your upper body swings a larger circle and tips the skis over onto their edges

Solution: Maintain handle control and keep tension on the rope. Maintain your body alignment and keep your stance tall. You already have some tension on the rope when skiing in the backward position. As you turn toward the front, pivot around your axis over the ski and minimize any pull from your upper body by keeping the rope handle close to your waist.

Basic Wake Tricks

To do a wake trick properly, you must perform the trick in the air with the skis not touching the water's surface. This is where the wake jumping skill described earlier pays off. If you have taken the time to learn how to edge up the wake and get the lift the wake provides, these tricks will be a breeze. If not, go back and learn how to jump the wakes and edge the trick skis with angulation to feel the top of the wake.

You may find it easier to do wake tricks by sliding the tricks over the wake and not getting air at first. Although you won't get any air on the trick, you will learn how to edge and pull at the same time. After successfully sliding the tricks, take a more aggressive edge tip and push off the wake's crest as you pull the handle into your hip and begin the rotation. The wake versions of the back, front, and reverses are done much like the basic versions, as follows:

1. Begin from the middle of the wakes or about 3 feet (1 m) outside the wake.

2. Edge up and through the wake, and push off the wake at the crest. Use the wake on the side that you are turning: the right wake for a clockwise turn and the left wake for a counterclockwise turn.

3. As you land the trick, get in a lower position on the ski by flexing your ankles and knees and dropping your hips into the wake. Try arching your back more to keep your head and chest up and in line with your rotational axis.

To develop a solid foundation, learn each wake trick in both the basic and reverse rotation from inside to outside the wake, outside to inside, and off both wakes. This is a great way to prepare for more advanced tricks. If you can do a wake trick and the reverse off both wakes and in both directions, you have a total of eight ways to perform each wake trick. For example, a wake back can be done (1) coming in toward the wake, (2) from outside the wake to inside and then going out the other wake, (3) from inside to outside and heading in the other direction, and (4) from outside to inside followed by inside to outside but turning in the opposite direction. The first two are regular backs, and the other two are reverse backs. It should be easier to do a back coming in than going out. This is because as you come into the center, the wake is not as steep as it is going out. Practicing all these variations is referred to as versatility training.

Transitional Tricks and Tips

Trick skiing has evolved dramatically in the last several years, not only from the standpoint of the availability of high-tech equipment, but also in the types of tricks being done. The popularity and creativity of wakeboarding has opened up a new world of ski tricks and moves that just a decade or two ago were thought too risky to put into a trick run.

Today, kids nine years and younger are cranking off flips and doing some advanced tricks that in the past weren't taught until much later. The learning has been accelerated by the crossover of skateboarders and snowboarders to water skiing. Because of this evolution, we will pass over some lower point tricks and move right into one-ski tricks.

Many skiers are instantly more comfortable on one trick ski than on two trick skis. This is sometimes due to a strong slalom background or surfing, skateboarding, or snowboarding experience. Whatever the reason, the key to success on one trick ski is the same as on two skis: learning to ride and control the ski from various positions and angles. The basic one-ski tricks are performed just like the two-ski versions with some small adaptations. We will cover those briefly before addressing toe tricks and more complicated tricks that will build your foundation before you start cranking off flips and body overs.

Do not try any advanced tricks if you don't have a trick release; no trick is worth blowing out a knee, tearing a hamstring, or getting caught in the rope. Releases can be purchased for all types of boats, and a split-pin release is the best choice because it is reliable. Use the release for toe, line, body over, and any wrapped tricks you do. Selecting a pin person is an important decision also. Choose someone who will pay attention and not be distracted or lose focus. You want your pin person to always err on the side of caution rather than cost you a season with an injury that could have been prevented.

One-Ski Skills

When skiing on one ski, you begin with the same skills you did on two skis—edging through and popping off the wakes and advancing on the boat. Practice the following skills to become more agile on your single trick ski.

Skill 1: Cutting and Edging on One Foot

Before taking your foot out of the rear toe binding, learn to get comfortable moving on one ski. Move as if you were slaloming or just playing around, changing directions as quickly as possible until you feel stable enough to aggressively cut and edge across the wakes. When you're ready, take your foot out of the rear toe binding and practice skiing on your stance leg. Doing so will improve your balance and stance and teach you how to tip the ski on edge and control the edge with your entire foot. You also need to learn angulation and how to position yourself over the ski for line and toe tricks.

The key to this skill is learning to tip the ski onto edge by putting more pressure on one side of the ski or the other. Try it first in the middle of the wakes. Initially, your body remains fairly aligned, or inclined, and the whole length of your body swings underneath your upper body, shoulders, and head. The movement is similar to a pendulum on a clock swinging from side to side. As you progress and are more skilled and able to edge aggressively, you can let the swinging occur from your hips on down to your feet. The ski will respond more quickly as you learn to aggressively set higher tip edge angles. Focus on trying to angulate by dropping your hips away from the handle as you set your edge as illustrated in figure 6.7.

Figure 6.7 Learn balance, angulation, and tipping control by practicing cutting and edging on one foot.

Skill 2: Cutting and Edging Using the Toe Strap

In this skill you will angulate the same was as in the previous skill but this time you will use the toe strap. Start by putting your foot in the toe strap on land just as you would with any new trick. Once you have the feel of how to pull the handle in, grab the rope in front of the toe strap, take your back foot out of the binding, and slide it into the toe strap. When you feel comfortable on land, you can take it to the water, which requires an added step of controlling the rope by slowly releasing with your hand and foot the extra rope you pulled in. You must stay on your toes and keep your knees bent during the entire process as demonstrated in figure 6.8.

Basic One-Ski Tricks

The tricks in this section are more similar to the two-ski versions than they are different. The concept is the same: start in a good, balanced stance with an aligned body position and advance on the boat with a strong, even pull on the handle to your waist. Initiate the turn with your hips and shoulders and release with the hand that is moving in the direction of the rotation. Then, reach with your free hand behind you toward the middle of your back for the handle. For the 360, you pass the handle and continue the rotation forward. Keep your eyes focused on the horizon and the handle close to your body. It is essen-

Figure 6.8 **Learning to tip the ski and edge with your foot in the toe strap is the first step to learning toe tricks.**

tial to maintain a proper body position while rotating around your body's axis throughout the trick so you do not fall. It is also part of the learning progression to become comfortable riding the single ski backward and learning to edge the ski across the wakes. This makes sense when you realize that almost half the time you are doing tricks you are in the back position. Remember to be patient and learn the reverses after you learn the basic tricks.

Half Wrap and Reverse

The half wrap and reverse half wrap are used to make more advanced tricks easier and quicker than the basic front to back and reverse. They are not that difficult to turn, but can be hard to hold because of the turning of the body and the pull from the boat. A great way to get the feeling of the slightly countered body position needed for riding and controlling the ski in this position is to first learn it on a wakeboard. The fins of a wakeboard keep the board tracking straight, and you can feel the correct position. These tricks are essential to master and open you up to some high-point tricks such as back to backs, 540s, and 720s.

Figure 6.9 **Keeping the handle low and close to the hips improves edge control.**

1. To learn the basic half wrap first, begin in the basic skiing position. Think of this trick as switching to riding fakie on a wakeboard.

2. Turn the ski to the back position in the direction of your front foot, and keep both hands on the handle. Hold the ski in the back position by using angulation of the hips, knees, and feet. As you can see in figure 6.9, the handle remains close to the body

with the knees and ankles well bent and the back and shoulders straight and level with the water.

3. Keep your upper body facing forward. The pull should be from the center of your body. This may require you to hold the handle behind your hips or lower back.

If you have trouble holding the position, try it outside the wake and use the wake to hold the ski in the backward position (left side for right foot forward). It is also helpful to put more weight on your back foot by flexing your knees to control the edge and get the ski to track better. If you are still having difficulty holding the half wrap position, try turning slower, so slow, in fact, that you almost break the trick into a side slide with an extra 90 degrees of rotation.

Another way to approach this trick is to turn the ski tip from the front (12 o'clock) to 2 o'clock position and progressively more until you are able to turn 180 degrees (6 o'clock). Holding this wrapped stance is not important at first; it is more about learning to pivot the tip of the ski until you are able to hold it in the back wrap position. You will know that this trick is solid when you can go outside the wake and to the back wrap. Outside the wake, everything is a bit more slippery, and the pull of the rope is from the side because you are not directly behind the boat. You can take it one more step and learn real control by edging the ski in the back stance through both wakes and back again in the other direction.

The reverse half wrap is done the same way as the half wrap, but in the opposite direction, or the direction of your back foot. This trick requires flexibility and a solid countered body position. Take your time to master this trick because the payoff in speed, strength, and balance is huge. Use the wake to help hold the position (right side for right foot forward). Concentrate on the handle. Keep it in tight to your body, and find a position that allows you to hold the handle low with the pressure on the hand that is closer to the boat.

Back to Back

Once you've mastered the half wrap and reverse half wrap, learning both surface and wake back to backs will be quick and easy. All you need to do is a half wrap and give a slight pull as you come forward and continue the rotation to the reverse half wrap. The movement is pivoting the ski by keeping both hands on the handle. The lower body pivots the full 360 while the upper body turns much less. Less body movement coupled with a strong starting position (aligned stance on the ski) results in quick, easy tricks that you can perform without having to pass the handle.

Some skiers find that back to backs are easier when they start from the reverse half wrap stance. If they are not able to hold the reverse back position, they can turn back and hold it momentarily before doing the back to back. If you take the time to learn to edge in the half-wrapped positions, the wake back to back and reverse will be a breeze to learn. The wake back to back and reverse while in a wrapped stance can be done without air, just sort of sliding over the wake and feeling yourself moving laterally as you cross the wake.

Getting air for any wake trick requires that you use your edging skill up the wake to track and establish a platform under your ski to push off from. If you

Figure 6.10 Learning to ski on edge up the wake correctly puts you in a balanced position to get air so you can tackle other tricks.

start to turn the ski too early, there will be no air and you will slide across the wakes. Tipping the ski on edge up the wake in any direction equals air as shown in figure 6.10.

Toe Turns

Always use a trick release and a competent pin person when learning toe turn tricks. The basic toe turns are the toe back, toe front, toe wake back, and toe wake front. It is imperative that you get comfortable riding your ski with your foot in the toe strap before trying these tricks. The secret, just like in all forms of skiing, is body position. Focus on flexing your ski leg by keeping it bent at the knee and ankle, and keep your weight over the center of the ski on the ball of your foot. Figure 6.8 shows the body position and stance for toe tricks. Keep your back straight and your shoulders level, and use your arms for balance. Let your arms hang down, and move your elbows out about 8 to 10 inches (20 to 25 cm) from your sides. Lift your forearms and the palms of your hands until they are about level with your elbows. This placement is not meant to be rigid; it is a starting point. Move your arms as needed to keep your balance.

Your rope leg should flex the way your arms do in handle tricks to advance on the boat. To learn handle control with your foot, bend your knee to pull in on the rope and hold it close to your ski leg; about 1 to 2 feet (30 to 60 cm) away is perfect. Then let it back out slowly. Learn to regulate the tension on the rope to maintain your balance. Extend and flex your rope leg to help keep you balanced as you ski in and out of the wake. Being too stiff with your rope leg makes you less stable. Allowing flexion and extension helps smooth out the ride.

You also need to learn to pull in and let the rope out with the toe strap. With your rope leg fully extended, pull your heel down closer to your stance leg by leaving your thigh up high and bending your knee. Another option is to pull the whole rope leg in and downward so that the rope foot is closer to the stance leg foot. For both of these movements, you should feel yourself advancing on the boat.

Toe Back

The toe back (see figure 6.11) is a good toe trick to learn first.

1. Start in a balanced stance directly behind the boat with your weight slightly forward on your toes, and pull in on the rope to advance on the boat.

2. Focus on keeping control of your rope leg as you pull in to advance, allowing the knee to bend. As always, keep your head and eyes looking on the horizon, keep your shoulders up, and keep your upper body as vertical as possible.

3. Keep yourself stacked by centering your weight over the ski during the turn and into the back position. Keep your head up during the turn.

4. At the end of the turn, maintain handle control by slowly letting the rope out with your leg.

Step 2 is sort of like standing on the ground with your rope leg out; as you pull in the rope leg and heel, you pull it toward the shin of the stance leg. On the water, advance doing the same movement, and you will be able to pivot the ski and maintain your rotational axis. A common pitfall of the toe back is that the turn and leg extension often happen together. You can resolve this problem by making a strong, smooth pull on the rope to advance on the boat enough so you can turn without tension on the rope and keep the rope leg knee near the stance leg knee.

Once you get to the back position, concentrate on maintaining a tall skeletal alignment of your body on your stance leg. Use your rope leg to regulate tension so you can maintain a balanced, correct position and get comfortable riding the

Figure 6.11 **The toe back.**

ski in the back position. Play around and feel how shifting your weight affects your pressure on the ski and how movement laterally affects how you tip the edge of the ski and how the ski tracks.

At the early stages inclining the body is what mostly affects edging and tipping. The low position of the rope lowers your center of balance so any movement of the hips and upper body greatly affects your balance, stance, and edging. Try edging by dropping your hip toward the wake and feel how the ski tracks. Notice how the ski feels when you are skiing backward while your rope foot is holding the handle. Let your rope leg extend and feel yourself having to counterbalance by bending at the waist. Practice letting your rope leg out and pulling it in so your rope foot is close to the calf of your stance leg. Play around in the back position and maybe even cross in and out of both wakes, so you learn to dynamically move around in the toe front and back positions and remain balanced.

Toe Front

The toe front (see figure 6.12) causes trouble for some skiers, but once you understand how to shift your weight and body position during the turn, it is easily mastered.

1. Start in a nice low position with your weight on your toes.
2. Make a firm pull in with your rope leg.
3. Lead the turn with your hips and shoulders and keep your stance leg flexed.
4. Reach forward to get weight on your ski leg toe as you come forward.

Some skiers have trouble with step 2. The common mistake is rocking your weight back onto your heel as you turn. Think about keeping your weight forward and on your toes as you rotate around. Your shoulders need to remain level with the water and can come forward slightly as you come forward.

Figure 6.12 **The toe front.**

Toe Wake Back and Front

The toe wake back and toe wake front are both easy tricks to do once you are comfortable with the surface tricks. Prepare for these tricks by learning to edge up and through the wakes in both the forward and backward positions. As with all wake tricks, it is usually easier to slide the tricks when first learning them. Here are the steps for the toe wake back (see figure 6.13):

1. Start in a low position on your ski by flexing your knees and ankles.
2. Hold an edge to the top of the wake.
3. Push off the wake as you pull on the rope, and initiate the turn as if you were doing a toe back.
4. Keep your back straight and core strong.
5. To prevent the ski from sliding out from under you as you land, keep your ski leg soft and flexed and your rope leg in close to your ski knee. Use your balance and tipping skills.

Figure 6.13 **The toe wake back.**

The key to this trick is learning the correct pull before the turn and edging to the top of the wake before starting the turn.

Many skiers learn the toe wake front faster than the surface toe front because the wake helps with the forward weight shift that is critical for mastering this trick. The steps for the toe wake front (see figure 6.14) are as follows:

1. Begin from the toe back position and outside the wake.
2. Set a firm edge toward the wake to keep tension on the rope.
3. At the crest of the wake, push off the wake with your ski leg to get lift and pull in on your rope leg to begin your rotation to the front.
4. Bring your shoulder forward to maintain vertical axis.
5. Spot the landing and maintain balance by flexing ski leg.

The most troublesome aspect of the toe wake front is learning to stay over the center of the ski and maintain your axis during the turn. This is overcome

Figure 6.14 **The toe wake front.**

by keeping the rope tight and close to the body. It sometimes helps to reach forward as you come forward to avoid falling backward.

Difficult Tricks Made Easy

The tricks that really fire up the crowd and get the screams from the fans are the big air tricks. Flips, body overs, and line steps are all awesome to watch, but don't let them intimidate you. Take it step by step and build on each trick. Stick to the tips you've learned so far, and you will save time. To land these awe-inspiring tricks, you have to be willing to go for it. Develop rock-solid fundamentals, and you will have what you need to land these big-point tricks.

Flip and Reverse

Trick ski flips have changed how skiers train and set up their runs. Once thought to be too risky, they are now the focal point of most competition skiers' runs. For safety and to give you the extra mental edge needed for committing to and going for the flip, wear a wetsuit, light vest, and maybe even a helmet. This will take the sting out of the falls and help you save energy for more attempts. You can do a standard flip (figure 6.15) or a reverse (figure 6.16). Here are the steps:

1. Begin a few feet (about a meter) outside the wake on the side of your front foot (right side of the wake for right foot forward and vice versa for left). Allow your arms to relax and straighten out.

2. Shift your weight over your front foot.

3. Make a slow, controlled progressive turn and set your edge by dropping your hip into the wake.

4. Maintain your edge and progressively cut harder all the way through the top of the wake. Keep your weight over your front foot.

5. As you pass through the top of the wake, push the tip of your ski backward away from the boat.

6. As the ski passes up and over your head, allow the rope to pull you and your ski around to the forward position.

7. Spot your landing by looking for the boat, and soften your knees for impact. Allow the ski to slide down the wake in the same direction that your cut began from.

Figure 6.15   The flip.

Figure 6.16   The reverse flip.

Ski Line Back

Ski line tricks are known as body overs because the body passes over the rope during the rotation. They evolved out of the old-school line step tricks that are used less frequently today. Here are the steps for the ski line back (see figure 6.17):

1. Begin in a relaxed, comfortable position with your arms out slightly and your weight over your front foot.

2. Take a slow, smooth edge up the wake as you begin a strong pull on the rope toward the hip that is closer to the wake. A key at this stage of the trick is to keep your shoulders up and even with the water's surface just as they are when you start the trick. Continue to pull the handle to the side of your hip all the way through the top of the wake. You should have both hands on the handle as long as possible to get a full advance on the rope.

3. Finish the pull to your hip as you edge through the top of the wake, let go of the handle with your outside arm, and pull your knees up to your chest.

4. At this point, your long, slow, progressive pull to your hip has advanced you far enough toward the boat that you should easily pass over the line without jumping or throwing your shoulders off axis.

5. Once you pass over the rope, begin to put your legs down, keeping your knees soft to absorb the impact of the landing. The handle needs to be as close to your hip as possible. Remember to keep your head and eyes up and focused on the horizon.

Figure 6.17 **The ski line back.**

Toe Wake Line Back

The toe wake line back is similar to the body over but is done from the toe position as shown in figure 6.18. You start with your body slightly behind a neutral position with your ski leg flexed at the knee and ankle and your rope leg out, but low. Follow these steps:

1. Take a slow, smooth edge toward the wake and begin to pull your rope leg toward your ski binding. This motion will also shift your weight and shoulders toward the boat. It is essential to keep your back straight and your head up.

2. Continue to pull your rope foot past your ski foot as you complete your edge to the top of the wake.

3. Maintain your edge and allow it to push you into the air and over the rope. Keep your head and shoulders up during your rotation. As you pass over the line, squeeze your rope foot and ski binding together.

4. Keep your knees soft and absorb the landing, letting the rope slowly pull you back to the boat.

5. Keep your eyes focused on the horizon and hold a normal toe back position.

Figure 6.18 **The toe wake line back.**

Trick Training Tips

As you try tricks that are more difficult, you will experience more falls and frustrations. Here are a few tips that will keep you feeling positive and making steady progress:

- Take the time to get really good at the skills in this chapter. This will result in quick successes and keep you from getting stuck on one trick because you have not perfected the fundamentals of the trick.

- Learn tricks in an order that is natural for you, but don't make the mistake of avoiding the reverses—they build strength for more advanced tricks.

- Take no more than five attempts on a new trick. This prevents you from getting into a rut or getting too frustrated with any one trick.

- Do whatever you need to do to stand up on the water and ride out the trick. Never throw the handle just because you are out of position. Fight until the rope is yanked out of your hand or the safety pin is pulled. You will be amazed at what you can pull out of, and you will learn how to ride and recover your balance quickly.

- Keep your sets to 15 to 20 minutes. Even though tricking requires less strength than slalom, when fatigue sets in, you lose some of your pull and balance. Concentration is essential to make progress in tricking, and usually it is waning after 20 minutes or so.

- Break every trick down to its basics, and think of the trick in that way when learning it. Learning a 540 front to back is simply a 360, which you can do easily, followed by a half wrap, which you can also do. Perform the trick this way with a pause and slowly shorten the pause and continue the rotation.

- Remember that any progress, at any point in your practice, whether it was what you are working on or not marks a good day of practice.

- See pages 164 to 167 in chapter 9 to learn about developing trick runs for competitions.

As in all sports, getting good at trick skiing is rooted in enjoying practice and having fun. Work is not work when you are enjoying it. In no event is this more true than in trick skiing. It takes time, dedication, and persistence combined with incredible balance and athletic ability to become a great tricker. If you set a goal of having fun while improving as well as reaching specific benchmarks such as new tricks, the hours on and off the water perfecting your movements will fly by.

Chapter 7

Jump Skiing

The current world record ski jump distance is 243 feet (74 m)! Years ago, when Freddy Krueger, the person who launched himself that incredible distance, and I lived at Bennett's Ski School, we could not comprehend anyone jumping such a distance. This alone tells you how far all aspects of jumping have come. Ski designs, speed suits, boats, and speed control systems have all had an impact on how jumpers attack the enchanted slanted. How we approach jump training and safety today has been adjusted to meet the evolving world of ski jump equipment and technology.

U.S. team coach Jay Bennett developed a jump learning system that eliminated the fear of cruising over the ramp, making learning how to jump like going down the bunny slope in snow skiing. This opened up jumping to a new set of skiers. Today kids and adults are learning how to jump and ride their jump skis correctly on a low ramp before moving to the full-sized ramp. By using a skills progression that first focuses on balance, edge control, pressure control, and strong body alignment to build an awareness of the interaction between the skis and body position, jumping is safer and more fun.

Body Position and Alignment

Figure 7.1 The proper body and hand positions for riding jump skis.

One of the funniest things I have ever witnessed behind a boat is the sight of an extremely well-known slalom skier attempting to ride jump skis. He looked like a giraffe on ice, struggling to find his balance and control the skis. You would think that someone who could run into 41 off would be able to rip it up on two skis. But, like many of us, as soon as he learned to get up on two skis, he tried the slalom, switched to one ski, and never looked back.

Few people ever really become comfortable on two skis, much less jump skis, which are wider, longer, and more difficult to control than combo pairs. Because of this, let's review the basic body position for riding jump skis. (If you happen to be a snow skier, the body position will be familiar. You ride jump skis in the same position.) Your head should be up, elbows in, ankles and knees bent, and feet shoulder-width apart (see figure 7.1). Hold the handle with your left hand under (palm up) and your right hand on top (palm down). Have your shoulders straight and your chest forward to keep your weight on the balls of your feet. Take the time to get your position set on land before going to the water. Once on the water, get in the correct position and start playing around on the skis.

Skill 1: Riding in Open Water

Riding your skis in open water and jumping the wakes will teach you the balance and edge control necessary for making your first jump (see figure 7.2). Spend several ski sets just riding your skis to get the feel of the

Figure 7.2 Your first jump is off the wakes to learn balance and edge control of jump skis.

correct body position. Learn to control your skis and your speed, both across the wakes and in the turns, by using the skis' edges. Each time you cross the wakes, load the skis and rope a bit more and feel where your balance point is (the position you need to be in to maintain your balance yet still edge the skis).

Try running the slalom course at a slow speed (15 mph, or 24 km/h) on jump skis. This drill is great for beginners just learning to ride jumpers. Jump skis glide more than combo skis do, and they turn differently, so body position is crucial. Get used to the feel of jump skis and start trying to jump the wakes by pushing with your feet right through your arches and keeping your skis shoulder-width apart. Keep your upper body still rather than swaying your arms or torso as you would to jump in other sports. You want to land with your center of balance over the middle of your feet as you would if you jumped down two steps, and to absorb the landing with your knees as you would if you jumped off a chair.

Gradually build confidence until you are be able to ride the skis with good body position and edge control. Five sets of six or so passes making eight wake crosses on each pass usually gets people comfortable with how to ride the jump skis with a level of proficiency worthy of a shot at the ramp.

Skill 2: Running Up a Hill

Before you ever actually hit a ramp, you will want to learn some movements and get a feel for the sensations you will have riding over the ramp and in the air. You can simulate these sensations by running up a hill or incline. When you run up a hill, you lean forward with your shoulders into the hill and put your weight on the balls of your feet. This is the same way you should go over the ramp. Just as you cannot run uphill while leaning back on your heels, you cannot go over a ramp in that position either. The tell, to use a poker term, is if your skis feel as though they are sliding out in front or if the handle comes toward your chest or chin when you cross the wakes or jump the ramp. When you are in the correct position, you will land in the middle of your feet with your knees flexed and be in a balanced, stable position with the handle close to your body.

Figure 7.3 Your skis should be flat and your weight should be evenly distributed when lining up a jump.

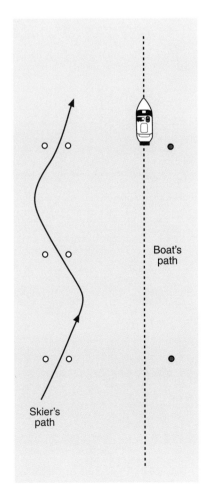

Figure 7.4 Practice the arc method using the slalom course.

Skill 3: Getting Flat With the Arc Method

The biggest key to a successful first jump is learning edge control of the skis. Part of learning edge control is learning to keep your skis flat with no edge as you ride over the ramp. When you are learning to jump for the first time, practicing riding flat with no tipping of the skis is more important than learning to ride the edges. You must line up to the jump with equal weight on both feet and the skis flat (see figure 7.3). If you feel tension on the rope or if you are fighting or resisting the pull of the boat, you will have unequal weight distribution on the skis and the skis will be on edge. This can cause the skis to slip out to the side.

The arc method requires some depth perception, timing, and practice, but it is the safest, quickest, and most successful way to learn to jump. You don't want to learn this at the jump, so we simulate a jump with buoys from a slalom course (see figure 7.4). Have the driver run the boat just inside the skier buoys. Pick out two gate buoys, pull out to the side of the boat, and then stop pulling and put the skis on a flat edge as shown in figure 7.3 (the skis are on a flat edge when equal spray is coming from both sides). Let the boat pull you back into the wakes and through the two buoys. Your path of travel will resemble an arc (thus the name of the drill). Imagine when you are going through the buoys that you are going over the ramp. Remember to think about holding a perfect body position and keeping the skis flat as you drift through the buoys.

Work on this skill until you have mastered it. It is worth the time and will give you added confidence. A little trick to check to see whether you are in correct position is to hook the rope to the trick release and have someone release the safety pin without warning as the boat pulls you back to the wakes. You will hardly notice you have been pinned if you are in the correct body position. You will simply glide to a stop and sink into the water. If your weight is back or if you are on edge, you will take a nice spill on your butt.

Ramping Up

With a solid sense of balance and tipping control, you are ready to feel weightless and fly through the air off the ramp. Have confidence, trust your preparation, and enjoy the ride. For your first attempt, simply do an arc over the miniramp (see figure 7.5). The correct path for the skier and boat are shown in figure 7.6. If you don't have a miniramp, ski off the side curtain of the full-size ramp (see figure 7.7). The correct path for the skier and boat are shown in figure 7.8. The process is the same with both. The phrase "knees, trees, freeze" can help you ride out your first jump. It means: keep your knees bent and soft in the proper position; keep your eyes and head looking up at the tops of the trees to help you maintain proper posture and balance; and freeze your skis and body once you get the skis flat. Do at least 10 jumps to increase your confidence.

Figure 7.5 Arc over the miniramp.

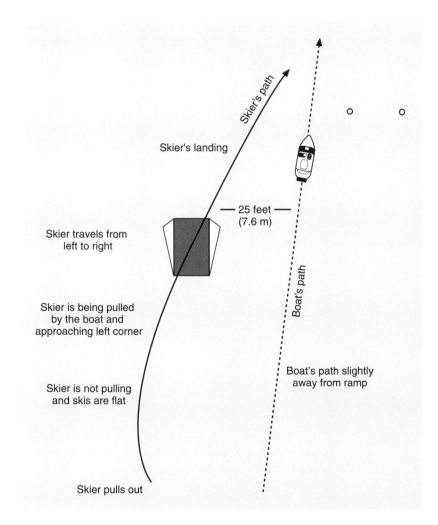

Skier's path

Skier's landing

— 25 feet —
(7.6 m)

Boat's path

Skier travels from
left to right

Skier is being pulled
by the boat and
approaching left corner

Boat's path slightly
away from ramp

Skier is not pulling
and skis are flat

Skier pulls out

Figure 7.6 Skier and boat paths for arcing over the miniramp.

Figure 7.7   **Skiing off the side curtain.**

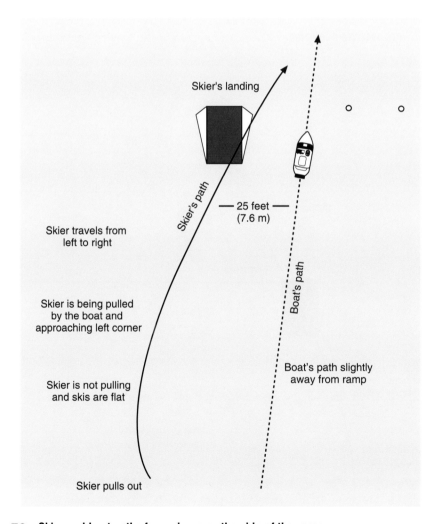

Figure 7.8   **Skier and boat paths for arcing over the side of the ramp.**

Your next challenge is to move up to the full-size ramp. This is usually an easy transition because you are confident and have mastered the correct arc technique by going over the miniramp. You can lessen the challenge of this transition by setting the ramp height at 3 1/2 to 4 feet (1 to 1.2 m) rather than the 5-foot (1.5 m) regulation height. Jump at the lower height for a few sets or until you are confident in your body position and landings.

Arc jumping from the full-sized ramp (see figure 7.9) is identical to jumping from the miniramp. The only differences are the amount of time you are on the ramp's surface and the height from which you land. To handle the increased time on the ramp, simply hold your body position longer. The impact on touching down from the full-size ramp will be greater than from the mini-ramp, so again, maintain your body position and do a proper arc over the ramp. The driver should follow the same path and speed used on the miniramp.

Landing from the higher height of the full-size ramp is easy to learn as well. Stand on a chair and jump down to get a feeling for the body position and body balance you need to land a jump and ride out. Your body needs to be slightly forward as your knees absorb the downward force. The feeling is similar to the body position you would use if you were bouncing on a trampoline and then wanted to stop quickly.

As the ramp height increases, the boat driver will run the same pattern, but at a slightly faster speed (2 mph, or 3.2 km/h, faster) to keep your tips from dropping and prevent falls on the ramp. You will do the same setup but pull out to a wider position for your arc. Get your skis flat, head up, and ankles bent, and ski over the ramp and stick a perfect landing. Keep a camera and photographer in the boat to catch this moment on film. You will be excited, to say the least, and the falls, if you have them, are always worth a laugh or two.

Figure 7.9 **An arc over a full-sized ramp set at its lowest height.**

Troubleshooting Beginning Jumps

Fall: Your skis slide out on the ramp.

Error: You are not on flat skies as you go over the ramp.

Solution: Make sure your skies are flat on the water; there should be no edge on the approach.

Fall: The ride over is fine, but you fall back onto your butt when you hit the water on landing.

Error: Your weight is on your heels, or you pulled the handle in to your chest.

Solution: Flex your knees and ankles to shift more weight to your toes, and press the handle down keeping your elbows at your hips.

Fall: You fall forward on landing.

Error: Your shoulders are too far forward, or your knees and ankles are not bent enough.

Solution: Straighten your back until your chest is up, but bend slightly at the waist to keep your weight on your toes. Lower your butt to the water by flexing your knees and ankles.

Edging Through the Ramp

Until now, you have been riding your skis to improve control and learn body position and arcing over the ramp on flat skis. This process teaches awareness and technical skills and builds strength—all of which you need to be more aggressive and get longer jump distance. Now it is time to put these elements together and learn how to edge into the ramp.

Jumping has evolved from the days when skiers were taught simply to cut across the wakes to build speed, flatten out before the jump, and kick it. Today, through the use of computerized training and biomechanical analysis, jumpers are taught to edge through the ramp to create and maintain more speed and create lift. You maintain the speed you generate by holding your direction across the wakes and over the ramp. When you hold that direction across to the base of the ramp, you get more lift because stronger resistance is created on the ramp and the boat gives you a stronger pull off the ramp and through the air. Think of the ramp in the same way as you think of the wake. You want to use the energy of the boat and ramp to assist you in getting lift.

Edging, or tipping the skis, across the wakes and into the ramp involves pushing forward with the knees and the ankles, away from the rope's pull on the edges of the ski, especially the right ski (see figure 7.10). You must also drop your hips away from the handle, angulating and pushing with the right knee to the left, away from the boat's direction. This position accentuates the edge and creates a stronger body position. This action is very similar to edging on snow skis. In addition, you must lead with the right ski into the ramp because it is doing most of the work and has more force on it. This dropping of the hip

Figure 7.10 Edging and holding direction into, through, and off the ramp.

and flexing of the knees and ankles (see figure 7.11) lowers your body's center of balance until you are in a sitting position with your thighs at a right angle to your lower leg. As stated earlier, you should strive to maximize the edging (i.e., put 90 percent of your weight on the right ski).

Your upper-body position is the same as it was when you were learning to ride over the ramp for the first time. Your shoulders and head are square to the skis, and your arms are low. The difference is the direction of the pull. You must concentrate on edging across the course and to the left by pushing your right hand toward your left hip. This action will keep your shoulders aligned with your skis and counteract the boat's pull away from your body. Your eyes need to be focused either on the top right corner of the ramp or on the horizon over that corner. The natural tendency is to look to the bottom left corner. This is a habit to avoid at all costs, so break it now if you are even thinking of looking down at the bottom left corner of the ramp.

Before going any further, let me address an issue that confused me until it was properly explained and demonstrated. We have stressed keeping your skis flat on the ramp as you go over so the skis don't slide out. Now we

Figure 7.11 Dropping your hips and flexing your knees and ankles lowers your body's center of balance as you edge into the ramp.

Checklist for Edging Through the Ramp

Just as any pilot goes through a checklist before and after a flight, you should do the same. Be sure to focus on the following tips before each flight you take off the ramp, and review them after the jump to evaluate whether you accomplished each one.

- ☐ Stay low in your skis with your weight on your toes as you approach the ramp.
- ☐ Focus your eyes to the top left corner of the ramp.
- ☐ Position the right ski slightly in front of the left as you set your edge to the ramp.
- ☐ Drop your hip and press your right knee into the ramp.
- ☐ Hold the handle low and position your elbows in at your hips.
- ☐ Place 90 percent of your weight on the right ski.
- ☐ Hold your direction across the course and edge through the ramp.

are trying to get you to edge through the ramp. How are you supposed to edge the skis through the ramp and not bust your bum? A quick, simple explanation is in the AWSA level III coaches manual: "The skis are on edge coming into the ramp and the skier is going from right to left. The angle of the skis themselves will match the angle of the ramp." Although this may not answer the question, the fact is, edging works, and it is much safer and more controllable than trying to ride flat skis while carrying speed into the ramp. Simply stated, the pull of the boat keeps the skis in the proper position as you edge through the ramp. If you don't have confidence or doubt this concept, watch the pros approach the ramp to help you visualize it.

Jumping Drills for Speed and Lift

Once people start jumping, they quickly get a hunger for more hang time and the adrenaline rush of going over the ramp and through the air. They want more speed, more height, and more of the addictive pop from the ramp. If distance is your desire, then speed and lift are your answers, but not just any type of speed. The speed you need is controlled speed. The concept of controlled speed begins with the fundamental skill of tipping for edge control and mastering how to ride the right ski into the ramp. Controlled speed means going fast the right way and at the right time and with the correct body alignment. With more speed, the danger increases, as does the fear. How do you learn to manage danger and fear? Be in control of their cause: speed. How do you control speed? Use the edges of your skis and your body alignment.

The next step is learning how to get lift. When you learned to jump, you were taught to freeze as you went over the ramp. This freezing was simply resisting the force of hitting the ramp. Now it is time to begin learning how to kick the ramp to get lift. The wake jump drill is a simple and easy way to learn the fundamentals of lift. The no-jump jumping and crane drills will teach you how to generate controlled speed through edge control.

No-Jump Jumping Drill

The next progression in learning to edge through the ramp is the no-jump jumping drill. (Before trying this drill, you need to be comfortable with riding in open water, so go back and work on the slalom course first if you need to.) The skier pattern for jumping is called a double cut: you pull up wide on the side of the boat on the left and then cut across the wakes up on the driver's side of the boat opposite the ramp and then cut back across the wakes toward the ramp. This is done to build speed into the ramp. Learning this pattern and how to control speed by properly tipping your skis on edge and using angulation and body alignment to maintain speed, control, and balance are the secrets to jumping far distances.

The first phase of the no-jump jumping drill is simulating the double-cut pattern without going over the ramp, which will help you learn controlled speed and body alignment. The no-jump can be done away from the jump course or by skiing the jump course but starting the pattern late so that when you turn toward the ramp, you are well past it (see figure 7.12). Pro jumpers do this drill endlessly. It is great for conditioning in the preseason and teaches control of the skis without worrying about timing or the ramp. The first few times you attempt this drill, you may be riding the edges of both skis. As you learn balance and alignment, you should emphasize cutting on the ski closer to the boat as you cross the wakes and maintain the position until you are even with the windshield alongside the boat. Work to get 90 percent of your weight on that ski as you cut through the wakes and up alongside the boat.

During a double cut, body position is crucial, as always. Your upper body should remain very still; most of the movement should occur in your ankles and knees as you extend your arms out and lean away from the boat by tipping your ski edges through the wakes (see figure 7.13). This is done by dropping your hip away from the boat and handle and angulating for balance, strength, and skeletal alignment. To get the feeling of dropping your hip, stand 1 to 2 feet (31 to 61 cm) from a wall or tree and get into basic ride-over position with your side facing the wall or tree. Now, act as though you were edging across the wakes. Drop your hip so both the hip and your shoulder are touching the wall or tree. Your shoulders must remain up and square to the skis, while your arms are low with your elbows to your sides and your hands together.

If you are having trouble holding this position on the water, lower the boat speed until you can maintain a perfect position while cutting through the wakes and up alongside the boat. Try 25 mph (40 km/h) to start. Pro jumpers are constantly working on dropping the hip and maintaining position across the course on one ski. Every jumper needs to master this skill.

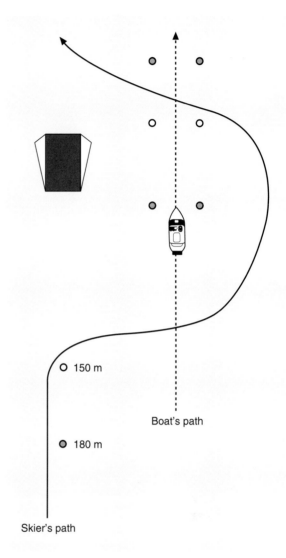

Figure 7.12 **The no-jump jumping drill simulating the double-cut pattern.**

  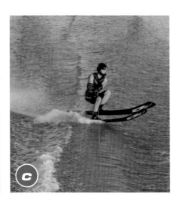  

Figure 7.13 The no-jump jumping drill emphasizes holding direction and keeping weight on the right-foot ski.

Crane Drill

The crane drill is so named because you will look like a crane standing on one leg. This drill is similar to the no-jump jumping drill, but it is more difficult. It will teach you balance and alignment as well as how to time your lean with the stretch of the rope and pull of the boat. Follow the same pattern that you did in the no-jump jumping drill, but this time lift the inside ski (the one closer to the boat as you pull out). For this drill, slow the boat speed down to a comfortable speed (20-25 mph, or 32-40 km/h), and pull out to the side of the boat. Make a slow, smooth turn, and lift the ski closer to the wake 1 foot (31 cm) off the water as you set your edge (see figure 7.14). Concentrate on staying low in your ski by bending your ankles and knees and dropping your hip. Keep the handle down and your elbows in. Keep pulling through both wakes and drop your hip even more as you come off the second wake. Maintain the crane until you are alongside the boat. Put the ski down, slow down, and make another smooth turn back through the wake on the opposite ski.

The crane drill is the best drill you can do to learn how to control your jump skis and drop your hip to attain the correct body position. As stated earlier, you should have 90 percent of your weight on your edging ski as you cross the wakes. This ski is known as the working ski. The crane stresses the working ski by forcing you to put 100 percent of your weight on it and still maintain a perfect edging position.

Figure 7.14 The crane drill teaches you how to control your skis and drop your hip to maintain balance and control.

Wake Jumping Drill

The wake jumping drill teaches you to use the energy of the wake to create lift. You can then transfer that skill to the ramp, converting the energy of the ramp into lift and distance. Start jumping one wake by pushing with your lower body with your skis together. Do not use your shoulders or upper body. Edge up the wake and extend your knees and ankles while keeping your upper body still and the handle in. (Using the wake for lift on skis is similar to doing it on a wakeboard, so the text on page 77 may be a helpful refresher.) For the wake and the ramp, focus on pushing up through the balls of your feet (as you practiced in running up the hill).

Now start from a wider position on the boat, take a harder edge tip, and carry more speed into the wake. Edge up the wake and push down on it by extending your legs at the top. You will begin to feel that the difference between a good lift and a flat lift relates to the tension on the rope and your ability to push down on the wake with tension or stretch on the rope. Keep doing this until you can clear both wakes in one jump. Once you can clear the wakes and have had a chance to get comfortable just going over the ramps, you are ready to transfer this skill to the ramp.

Single-Wake Cut

With the single-wake cut, jumping puts on a new face, and the real fun begins. You see the ramp from a new angle, one that may make you question whether you can edge over it without skiing over the side curtain. Remember that jumping is a smart skier's event, not a crazy skier's challenge. When you challenge the ramp, you must be confident and smart in your approach. But have no fear. If you have done the drills and taken the time to learn how to ride your jump skis, you have every reason to be confident about improving your distances because you have built a foundation that will take you far.

The first word to remember from this point on about your jumping career is *progressive*. You must learn to start smoothly and slowly and build your speed as your edge gets progressively stronger all the way through the ramp. It sounds easier than it is. When you are on the water, things seem to move a little quicker, and you may be tempted to rush a bit. Calm down, slow down, and stay progressive with your edge. Now let's hit the wedge!

Have the driver run the boat parallel to the ramp, splitting the left side of the ramp and the 15-meter buoy as shown in figure 7.15. The ramp is set at 5 feet (1.5 m), and the boat speed should be in the 24 mph (39 km/h) range. Position yourself just outside the left wake, and assume the basic body position, just like in arcing. Focus your eyes on the top left corner of the ramp, and take a progressive edge up through the middle of the ramp (see figure 7.16). The key is to maintain a strong edge, correct body position, and good control throughout the edge and over the ramp.

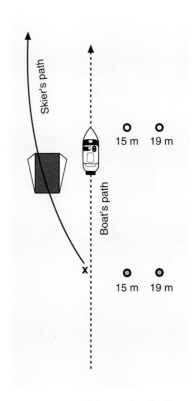

Figure 7.15 **To learn the single-wake cut, first practice passes with the boat driver splitting the ramp and the 15-meter buoy.**

Figure 7.16 **A single-wake cut teaches proper alignment and position at the most critical part of the approach to the ramp.**

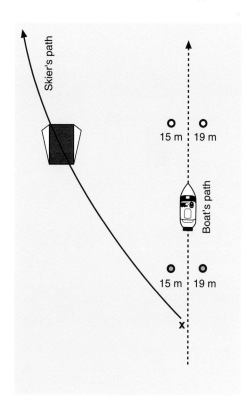

Figure 7.17 **The single-wake cut with the driver of the boat following the split.**

After a few sets using the initial boat position, have the driver move the boat away from the ramp in 2-foot (61 cm) increments until he is driving what is known as a split—splitting the 15-meter and 19-meter buoys as shown in figure 7.17. This wider position will force you to maintain an edge longer and allow you to generate more speed into the ramp. You will feel the increased distance and begin to feel the float that is so addictive as you gain more confidence and take a harder edge and more speed into the ramp.

If you have trouble landing or riding out your jumps, a few tips can help. If you find you are falling back on landing or the handle is coming up around your chin or chest in the air, one of two things is happening. Either you are flattening out your skis before you hit the ramp, causing you to pull up on the handle to keep it tight, or you are edging with your weight shifted back on your heels. In both cases, concentrate on keeping the handle down and your elbows in to your sides as you press your right knee into the ramp.

The final phase of the single-wake cut is to increase your speed. Until now, you have been learning to generate your own controlled speed by edging your skis. Now it is time to adjust to the feeling of approaching at a faster boat speed. The driver should increase the boat speed in small increments (1-2 mph, or 1.6-3.2 km/h) and maintain the same boat pattern. You are still in charge of generating your own speed, but now the boat will assist you by giving you greater resistance to push against through the ramp. The body position and cutting position remain the same.

When increasing speed, most problems arise from lack of control, which causes the loss of the edge into the ramp. Another problem is that the increased power of the boat pulls you off your edging ski. If this happens, slow the boat speed down 1 mph (1.6 km/h) and try it again. The idea is to practice habits that are correct and build on these strengths. Don't be too proud to slow the speed down to maintain proper body position and gain controlled speed. Always be a smart jumper, and you will go far. Focus on learning a progressive edge with controlled speed, and you will have a longer jumping career in both distance and time.

Advanced Jumping

If you have taken your time and mastered all of the preceding skills, you should now be jumping in the 50- to 80-foot (15 to 24 m) range on a 5-foot (1.5 m) ramp at 30 to 32 mph (48 to 51 km/h). If you are not, go back and learn to jump at least those distances before using the advanced techniques presented in this section. Jumping can get dangerous if you have not taken the time to master the art of controlled speed. Proceed with caution and make sure you have the fundamentals mastered, or you will pay the price and end up with a neck that doesn't want to turn and a back so sore it hurts to lie down or worse.

Top jumpers try anything and everything to gain an extra foot or two on the competition. Speed suits, new ski designs, and different positions in the air are all having a great impact on the length and consistency of big jumps. Jumps of 200 feet (61 m) and more have become commonplace on the pro tour, but fans never tire of watching the awesome speed, explosive lift, and heavenly float attained by today's best. What are their undisclosed secrets?

Extra-Distance Gear

These items provide stability, speed, strength, and safety so you can be more aggressive in jumping. Refer to page 10 of chapter 1 to see a skier geared up in the appropriate equipment.

- **Arm sling.** An arm sling is essential to help you with position and control. The purpose of the arm sling is to concentrate the pull of the boat at the center of your body. This creates a stronger position and helps maintain body position through the wakes and in the air. The sling is responsible for that kitelike lift that adds distance to the jump by pulling you up as you get the pull from the boat during the first half of the flight off the ramp. You must still resist the pull from the boat with your back and arms to prevent being pulled out the front, but the sling makes it easier to hold on to the handle and pull of the boat.

- **Speed suit.** Speed and lift are the two primary forces that create big distance, but a third factor, drag, must be overcome to attain your full potential. The speed suit is designed to reduce drag. Speed suits have been around since the 1980s, but today they seem to be standard issue rather than just an experimental piece of equipment. By reducing drag through the wakes and in the air, you overcome the one force that can slow you down. A great deal of experimentation continues with speed suits. Top skiers are trying new materials and shapes to achieve a more aerodynamic flow during flight.

○ **Jump skis.** The biggest innovations in jumping today are happening with skis. The big dogs of jumping are going wild, experimenting with longer skis, wider tips, different rocker patterns, side cuts, and tapers that radically change the turning and edging characteristics of the skis. It seems to be paying off: record jumps are occurring at every level with a greater frequency than ever before.

○ **Helmet.** A helmet is a must-have for all phases of jumping. *Never jump without one!* Find one that fits snugly and will not bucket, or fill with water upon landing.

Three-Quarter Cut

With all the right gear, the ability to control your speed, and solid technique riding your skis, you may believe you can go farther. You may even be able to see the 100-foot (31 m) buoy just in front of you when you land your current single-wake jumps. This is the most dangerous point in your jumping career because you have just enough talent, strength, and ability to hurt yourself if you push beyond your limits. In fact, some top coaches keep their students jumping with a single-wake cut for a full season or more to ensure that they can control their skis and speed. This may seem like a long time, but the skiers who take the time and learn to ride their skis end up improving the quickest.

The next phase is learning to jump from a wider position known as the three-quarter cut. The three-quarter cut should begin as nothing more than an extended version of the single-wake cut. The difference is that you start from a slightly wider position—10 feet (3 m) outside the right wake rather than the left wake (see figure 7.18). Keep the boat speed and path the same as those you used for your single cuts (28-30 mph, or 45-48 km/h). The same principles of progressive edging and controlled speed apply, except now timing is more involved.

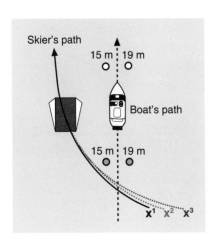

Figure 7.18 The skier and boat path for the three-quarter cut.

To help adjust to the new timing without the worry of going over the ramp, do the no-jump jumping drill with one small addition. Set out two buoys about 12 feet (3.7 m) apart and away from the ramp. These buoys represent the ramp. On a jump course, use the second set of timing buoys to simulate the ramp. (If you do not have a jump course set up, run the boat in a straight line about 50 feet, or 15 meters, outside the buoy closest to the boat.) Pull out 10 feet (3 m) outside the wake, assume the correct body position, and focus on the left buoy, which represents the top left corner of the ramp. Don't worry about the wakes; let the boat slowly pull you over them as you set a soft edge. As you come off the second wake, you should be near the same position you have been taking on your single cut. Drop your hip and edge up and through to the middle of the buoys.

Try this until you are comfortable, confident, and in control of your body position, skis, and speed. Once you feel you are ready, take it to the ramp with confidence, concentrating on holding your edge as you drop your hip off the wake into the ramp. Stay calm and be smart, and you will soon be jumping 100 feet (30 m) or more.

Once you get solid at jumping from this wider position, move out a little farther to about 20 feet (6 m) outside the wakes and go through the same process. Now do the same thing from 30 feet (9 m). The farther you move out, the more speed you will carry into the base of the ramp, and the more critical body position and timing will be. You should be able to generate 80 to 90 percent of your maximum distance from a three-quarter cut, so you should spend a great deal of time mastering this technique. Take the time needed to become aware of your location in relation to the boat and the ramp. Develop a sense of timing and stay safe and in control of your speed and position. If things aren't right, then pass!

Up until now you have been running the boat between, or splitting, the jump course buoys. As you learn to take a stronger edge and ski across the course more, you will arrive at the ramp earlier. You can keep your turn at the same location and

Figure 7.19 **The three-quarter cut path.**

get back into a full cutting position by beginning to move the boat out wider toward the right-hand side of the course. Move it out in 1- or 2-foot (31 or 61 cm) increments until you find a spot that is comfortable for you to take a full, strong edge into the ramp as shown in figure 7.19.

No matter how much you practice, some approaches to the ramp won't be quite right. In these instances, you need to pass on the jump for safety. You pass by letting go of the handle when you realize this will not be a safe jump and ski around the left side of the ramp. Avoid hitting any portion of the ramp by hopping over the corner if need be. If you are early into the ramp, pass. If you are late into the ramp, pass. If you are on your heels, pass. If your skis are behind you, pass. If you don't have confidence, pass. Do not try to salvage a bad start or edge. By learning to pass, you will stay safe and practice good habits of edging and turning slowly.

Because passing on purpose teaches bad habits, you should pass on a jump only when safety is an issue. The secret to good jumping is learning to edge through the ramp. When you pass, you usually stop pulling just after the wakes and let go of the handle and ski around the ramp. This is the opposite of what you want to practice doing. If your approach is unsafe and you don't feel confident, you should pass, but be sure to take the jump when things are good so you can gain experience and confidence with each jump.

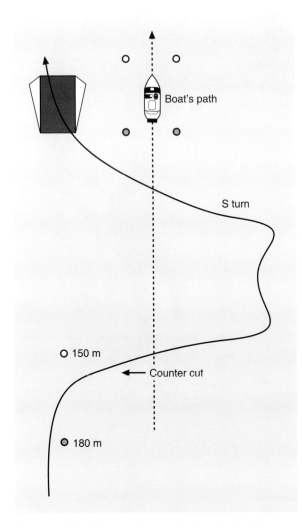

Figure 7.20   Skier and boat paths for the double cut.

Double Cut

As stated earlier, you should be able to achieve nearly all of your distance from a three-quarter cut. The rest comes from the double cut. The purpose of the double cut is to position the skier out wider to create more angle across the wakes and generate more speed into the ramp. The skier and boat paths for a double cut are shown in figure 7.20. The increased angle and speed equal greater distance. The trade-off is consistency. The wider you get on the boat, the more critical the timing of the turn and cut becomes.

To perform the double cut, you must learn how to make the counter cut. The counter cut is different from the cut to the ramp. Because its only purpose is to position you wider on the boat, a more leveraged position, similar to that used in slalom, is called for. The timing of the turn for the counter cut is assisted by the 500- and 600-foot (152 and 183 m) buoys. You pull out to the left side of the boat and use a snowplow position (as with snow skiing, point the tips of your skis together to slow down quickly) to control your speed for the turn. Once your skis are turned, apply pressure to the left ski and pull through the wakes across the course and up alongside the boat. When you have achieved your maximum width, you need to pull the handle up and across your body. This extra action gives you additional speed and advances you farther up on the boat.

As you glide down the lake, you prepare for the next phase of the double cut, the turn. The double-cut turn is different from the three-quarter-cut turn. Because you are farther up alongside the boat, you cannot make the same turn without creating slack in the rope or dropping back to a narrower position. You must learn the S turn to solve this problem (see figure 7.21). The S turn begins by letting your

Figure 7.21   The S turn for the double cut.

left arm extend out during the glide. As you glide, rotate your left hip away from the boat. This action edges you away from the ramp and keeps the rope tight. Now shift your weight to your right ski and make a slow rotation with your right hip back to the handle. At this stage it is critical that you maintain your forward water speed and ski through the turn as you do in slalom skiing. This will help you avoid creating pull from the boat until you are fully rotated and set in an aligned position that allows you to hold the acceleration of the boat.

Your eyes should be fixed across the course and not on the ramp, your knees should be flexed, and the handle must be down and in near your body. Set your edge and hold your direction across the wakes as you have been doing with the three-quarter cut. It will be slightly more difficult to hold the edge because of the increased angle. If you are having trouble, back up or spend more time practicing the drills you learned in the earlier sections.

A slow rotation toward the ramp while keeping your speed as high as possible is key. This sounds easy, but when you are looking across the course and see the side curtain of the ramp, you have a tendency to rush everything. You can overcome this by using a cut and pass drill, in which you make a turn and cut as if you were actually going to hit the ramp but let go at the last possible second and safely go around the ramp. This helps you learn the timing of your turn without worrying about the ramp. Use this drill to see the new perspective of the ramp and boat and make any adjustments.

Raising the Ramp and Getting Lift

Until now you have been jumping on a 5-foot (1.5 m) ramp and have mastered all of the skills we have discussed. The next step is to raise the ramp to 5 1/2 feet (1.7 m) to feel extra lift and distance. Conquer the bigger ramp with the same methods you used to master the 5-footer. Raise the ramp in 2- to 3-inch (5 to 7.6 cm) increments and begin with a single cut. Once you get the feel of the extra incline, move to a three-quarter cut, and so on. The process remains the same until you are jumping on the pro tour with the 6-foot (1.8 m) wall.

Safety Crush

You have just made a perfect turn and are right where you want to be. You set your edge and get a burst of speed that rockets you across the course and through the wakes. You look at the ramp as you cross the wakes and—*Oh, no.* You feel yourself rock back onto your heels. This sets off your safety alarm system: *Abort!* You know this is a bad position to be in, but it is too late to pass. What do you do? If you hit the ramp, it could mean a painful or dangerous back or neck injury. The ramp is right there. You keep your head on straight and do a safety crush. Good decision!

The safety crush is a skill an advanced jumper must perfect to guarantee a lengthy career. If you find yourself in a less-than-desirable position and believe that trying to spring or resist the ramp will result in a crash, simply absorb the force of the ramp by allowing your legs to buckle under your body. Like all skills, you must practice this until it becomes natural and controllable. The crush should be instinctive whenever you are in a poor position approaching the ramp.

Figure 7.22   From knees, trees, and freeze to fly.

A drill that is sometimes helpful in learning the timing of the kick at higher speed without the effort and danger of a full cut is the high-speed flyover. Have the driver drive 5 to 10 mph (8 to 16 km/h) faster than your normal jumping speed, and take a single-wake cut at the ramp. This will help you do two things: adapt to setting an edge at higher speeds, and react to the ramp as you approach it with greater speed.

What advice do the pros have? When Freddy Krueger and I were on the U.S. team together and training for the World Championships, he said that 70 percent of jumping is having the guts to wait later and cut harder; the other 30 percent is using your brains so you stay alive. The top jumpers stress the same things: stay aggressive, edge through the ramp, keep your weight on your right ski, and keep your eyes and head up. The results are jumps like the one in figure 7.22. When you have developed a solid foundation and the proper skills needed for edging through the ramp, the same things apply to you.

Troubleshooting Advanced Jumps

One great advantage jumpers have over those in other events is that they get three attempts to go as far as they can. This means you have to be able to diagnose your problems on the water, make adjustments, and cut at the ramp again. Following are a few common errors and corrections to help you make adjustments.

Problem: Your skis slip out to the left on the ramp.
Cause: This is a result of flattening your skis at the base of the ramp and letting the boat pull your shoulders toward the boat.
Solution: Concentrate on edging through the ramp and resisting the boat's pull by keeping the handle down and your shoulders parallel with your skis.

Problem: Your skis split on the ramp.

Cause: If your skis are too far apart as you approach the ramp, your legs are in a weak position. This prevents you from resisting the ramp; instead, the impact force of the ramp causes your skis to split apart.

Solution: Get your skis closer together during the cut to the ramp so your legs are in a stronger position to push off the ramp.

Problem: You lose control when crossing the wakes.

Cause: It is easy to lose angle through the wakes because that is where the strongest pull from the boat is. You may be shifting your weight to the left ski for balance across the wakes, but that is the opposite of what you should do.

Solution: Push your skis, especially the right one, onto edge more by driving your right knee down and across the course toward the ramp.

Problem: You inadvertently crush your lower body on the ramp.

Cause: The lower-body crush is caused by having your knees flexed too much at the base of the ramp. The impact is so great that your legs are not able to respond quickly enough, which causes them to buckle underneath you.

Solution: Get your knees in the proper 90-degree bend so they can resist the ramp with a quick extension of the legs; this results in a springing lift off the ramp's surface.

Problem: Your upper body crushes.

Cause: Having your legs too straight at the base of the ramp with your shoulders down and back hunched over causes the lifting forces to be absorbed by your upper body. This is also a dangerous position because it can lead to the dreaded OTF (out the front), the most painful of all jump crashes.

Solution: Flex your knees more, and keep your back straight by pulling the handle down lower and closer to your body. Keep your head up, and focus your eyes on the left corner of the ramp or on the horizon as you approach the base of the ramp. Your upper body must remain calm, still, and erect so the explosive power of your legs can lift your entire body up and off into flight.

Problem: You slip backward.

Cause: The "out the back" is caused by having your weight on your heels or sitting back too far as you approach the base of the ramp. This often happens when you are too early and flatten your skis off into the ramp.

Solution: If you are early and are flattening out your skis, turn later and slower and hold your edge through the ramp. Always shift your weight to your toes before you start your turn, and press your knees and ankles into the skis as you initiate the turn.

Chapter 8

Off- and On-Water Practice

s my former coach, Jay Bennett, likes to say, "There are no shortcuts to championships." Training and preparing yourself physically and mentally off and on the water is how you earn the right to win. The time I spent with Jay set me up to accomplish some things that I never dreamed were possible when I first started working with him. One night at dinner, Jay and I were talking about why the U.S. team he coached had lost the world championships. At the end of the conversation, Jay said, "We needed a slalom specialist like you." Until that moment, I hadn't thought I was good enough to make a U.S. team. Jay's comment made making the team seem possible, and I decided to go for it. Being selected to represent my country as a member of the USA Water Ski team for the world championships and winning a gold medal are two of the highlights of my life.

The point of the story is this: What you do off the water (who your coach is, who you train with, how you develop your skills mentally and physically) is as critical as the practice you do on the water. This chapter shows you how to set yourself up for success through your off- and on-water training.

Off-Water Training

Earlier chapters addressed some forms of off-water training and preparation, such as getting the right equipment and getting physically fit. This section addresses other things you need to do to prepare for success. You may have heard the saying "Prior planning prevents poor performance." A positive rewording of this would be: "Prior planning precedes the podium."

Find the Right Coach for You

One of your first tasks is to find a coach or training partner who understands your skiing or wakeboarding style and what you are working on, and who cares about seeing you accomplish your goals. Only a handful of people fit into that category for me. Training both on and off the water with these people always affirms what I think and feel on the water. They help me accurately assess my skiing and my training.

Before Jay, Steven Schnitzer taught me how to ski from a technical standpoint and how to set up my ski to perform in sync with my style, strengths, and skill level. In a little under two years under Schnitz, I went from a 32-off weekender to a 39-off top-10-in-the-world skier. To this day, Schnitz is the person I call when I'm setting up a ski and trying to get it to work right. He understands when I explain what I feel and see on the water. When I am struggling with my ski setup, I call Schnitz so frequently that my ski partners tease me about it. Other important people have influenced my skiing as well. The two years I spent training with Andy Mapple, as well as the seasons I trained with Doug Ross and Richard Kjellander, were invaluable in teaching me how to train to compete and win. My training partners today, Matt Heinz and Steve Bauman, know me well enough to predict what I am thinking and feeling on the water. They also know what to do to get me focused leading up to competition.

As an athlete, you must constantly tweak your training program to address your weaknesses, and it is nearly impossible to do it alone. You should select a coach with the same care you would use to select a surgeon. You would not choose someone to operate on you based on personality or a fancy office. Similarly, you should find a coach who can assess your skills and qualities, make a diagnosis, and give you the prescription that is the best path for your success. As the team leader, the coach should have a fundamental knowledge of sports medicine and sport science to help you avoid injury and maximize your time on and off the water. Most important, your coach must be able to connect and communicate with you to bring out your best.

I credit Chet Raley, one of the best coaches at making that connection with skiers and boarders, with helping me win a gold medal at the Pan American Championships in Chile. In the weeks leading up to the tournament, I was behind in my training and not skiing very well. The pressure was mounting, I was struggling, and I had no confidence in my training and technique. To make a bad situation worse, two days before we left for Chile, my ski broke. After scrambling to get a new ski setup, I boarded the plane to Santiago a total mess. Chet, one of the team coaches, and I talked about the situation on the long flight from Miami. I could tell that he understood what I needed.

When we landed, he simply said, "Don't worry. We will get you set up to win." Then, we went out to a practice lake and went to work. Rather than trying to get me to ski my best scores, Chet considered the competition, the conditions, and the pressure that everyone felt in representing their country in international competition. He said, "You need to run three or four at 39 to win; let's get the ski there." That took some pressure off me and got me focused on something I knew I could get done in the little time we had. I made it through the qualifying round and ran three at 39 in the final to win the gold for the United States. Without a smart, insightful coach at that event, I am not sure I would have made it out of the qualifying round.

Surround Yourself With Support

Your support team members may work behind the scenes and rarely see you ski. My wife Yvette takes care of our four children while I am off at tournaments and puts a banner across the front of the house when I come home with a win or a record. Your support team can be as simple as your spouse or parents, or as complex as an entourage of physicians, therapists, trainers, physiologists, biomechanists, sport psychologists, sport nutritionists, and coaches. Whoever constitutes your support team, be sure they instill confidence and provide encouragement and motivation. This will help you focus on what you need to get done on the water. The key element of a support team is communication, and the coach is the conductor of the orchestra.

Simulation Skill Development

Simulation drills are sometimes referred to as static exercises, dry land practice, or stationary drills. The idea is to go through the motions on land as if you are on the water. Athletes in many sports get ready and mentally alert by simulating skills while awaiting their turn to perform. Developing your simulation skills helps you learn to feel the movements you make on the water.

Dry land practice is also an essential way to receive effective coaching. Practicing out of the water allows you and your coach to see your movements, analyze them, and make subtle changes on the spot. Your coach can take a hands-on approach to help you learn the correct biomechanics before you take to the water. The result is that you go to the water with a specific feeling to imitate, maximizing the use of your time on the water.

Movement Skill Development

Learning how to tip your skis or board in a balanced and coordinated manner is essential. The subtle feel of the foot motion and pressure you apply to start these movements is difficult to learn. The following two drills will give you the feel of using your entire foot for balance as well as simulate on-water movements.

Figure 8.1 Rope walking can help you develop foot awareness and balance.

Figure 8.2 Tracing the rope with your foot helps develop foot awareness.

Drill 1: Rope Walking

Walking on rope develops foot awareness and helps you sense balance through the length of both feet. For this drill, you will need a 5- to 10-foot (1.5 to 3 m) length of ski rope. Stretch the rope in a straight line across a firm, smooth floor. In your bare feet (or with socks on if the rope hurts your feet), walk forward and backward on the rope in a heel to toe manner (see figure 8.1). Keep your eye focused on the horizon, and use your sense of touch to move along the length of the rope. Counterbalance with your hips and arms to maintain balance. You will feel the tipping movements of your feet as you try to maintain balance.

After you get the feel of walking on the rope, you can try a few variations of this drill. Leave the rope straight and try walking backward. Then, try walking forward or backward as you did previously, but this time with your eyes closed. Next, arrange the rope in an S-curve pattern and use your feet to feel your way forward and backward along the rope.

Another option is to lay the rope in a curve or a circle, depending on the length of your rope. The pattern of the curve or circle should be wide enough for you to stand on the handle (or in the middle if your rope is longer) on one foot and comfortably reach the rope with the other foot. Trace the rope with your free foot (see figure 8.2), and then switch your feet and repeat the exercise. You can complete various versions of this technique. You can follow the rope with your toes, your heel, your arch, or even the edge of your foot on the little toe side.

Drill 2: Board Balancing

If you don't mind investing in another piece of equipment, the Indo Board Balance Trainer is a great tool not only for developing core strength but also, more important, for feeling and learning the interaction between tipping for edge control and balance in all planes of motion. The Indo Board Balance Trainer is a deck that sits on top of an inflatable cushion, creating an unstable surface that offers a real balance challenge. Follow the instructions for inflating the cushion to the level that's right for you. Then, position the cushion beneath the board and work on the balance exercises that come with the Indo Board. You can also find them at www.indoboard.com.

Later, after you have had the chance to practice on the Indo Board, you can take your training a step further by using just the cushion under your ski or wakeboard. Whether you are still on the Indo Board or have moved onto to your ski or wakeboard, add your bindings to simulate the foot position you use when on the water. Most important is that you look straight ahead and maintain a dynamic balanced position on the Indo Board or your board or ski with a bent-knee stance (see figure 8.3). Be sure to bend at the knees, not at the waist, and keep your head and shoulders up. As you bend your knees, you will feel your toes and the balls of your feet pushing to level the Indo Board, ski, or wakeboard so you maintain balance. Your upper body, head, shoulders, and arms should remain calm and still. Only your legs and ankles should move. You should also be sure to engage your core muscles. If you have trouble maintaining a dynamically balanced position or keeping your upper body still, you may need the help of a spotter, or you may need to hold on to a stationary object.

Once you have the feel of dynamic balance, you can work on tipping and countering movements in each plane of motion depending on the foot alignment of the event you're training for. For all events, you can feel the countering movements as shown in figure 8.4. For wakeboarding, you will feel heel-side and toe-side tipping (see figure 8.5) as well as fore–aft balancing. In slalom, you will feel on-side and off-side tipping and fore–aft balance. Practicing in hard-shell bindings (rather than barefoot or in athletic shoes) will give you a better feel for how your feet move. You will feel the body alignment angles and positions you need on the water. These exercises help you develop the small muscles you need and stretch the muscles and ligaments so you can move your body into correct alignment on the water.

Figure 8.3 The Indo Board is great for building strength and for helping develop dynamic balance.

Figure 8.4 You can feel proper counterbalance movement on the Indo Board.

Figure 8.5 The Indo Board can help wakeboarders learn *(a)* heel-side tipping and *(b)* toe-side tipping.

Drill 3: Trampoline Simulations

A trampoline in your backyard is a great place to practice movements for every event on the water. Learning to jump up and down and side to side and to maintain dynamic balance develops spatial awareness, is fun, and transfers to movements behind the boat. A trampoline offers a soft landing for learning tricks and reduces the risk of injury when attempting advanced moves. Plus, if you don't pull off the move, you don't have to wait in the water or burn gas as the boat swings back to pick you up. Jumping on a trampoline with a wakeboard strapped on is difficult and could cause injury. To simulate the board, try shaping a small board from soft foam such as that used to make boogie boards.

For tricking and wakeboarding, tie a rope to a nearby tree or other stationary object to simulate the boat tow and give the rope some tension so you can create rotation. If nothing is nearby to use as a tie-off point, someone standing on the ground can hold the rope. Hold on to the rope handle and practice your moves. Start with easy tricks such as 180 and 360 rotation and build up to more complex tricks such as the body over shown in figure 8.6, and focus on the intricate movements and the positions needed to perform the movements correctly. Progressively increase the energy of the movements and the height of the jumping actions needed to maintain balance.

Slalom simulation on a trampoline is a great way to get a feel for the counterbalancing movements you need to use in turning the ski. You can also learn how to reweight the ski in transition. Start by bouncing side to side with your head and upper body calm and still (see figure 8.7); then start going harder and harder to the side with your feet. Notice your knee movements and the angles of your lower body to your upper body. This is the identical feeling you will have when you are creating proper load behind the boat and when you release from the boat as you advance into the turn.

Figure 8.6 Trick skier learning a body over on the trampoline.

Figure 8.7 Jumping side to side on a trampoline simulates the knee flexion and extension used in slalom skiing.

For jump skiing, you can use a trampoline to learn proper air position and work on your landings. For proper air position, practice the feel of pushing out over your skis in the air as shown in figure 8.8. When focusing on landing, work on landing and absorbing the impact properly as shown in figure 8.9.

Figure 8.8 Practice the proper air position for jump skiing.

Figure 8.9   Jumping off a trampoline simulates how to land in a balanced position jumping off the ramp.

Managing Injuries

What is the single greatest inhibitor of improvement in any sport? Without question or debate, it is injury. No matter how good you are or want to be, nothing will prevent you from improving more than injury. If a minor injury is not properly attended to and allowed to heal, it can produce a domino effect that can derail a career. The impact is often beyond physical. When you have an injury, you can lose confidence in the injured area and want to protect it. Because the injury can't take as much stress, you don't push it. This can cause reinjury or an injury to another part of the body as a result of overcompensation.

Learning to manage injuries properly is essential and simple. To rebuild your confidence and get back on the water as fast as possible following any injury, follow this three-step procedure:

1. Protect the injured limb, joint, or muscle from stress immediately following the breakdown. Use the PRICE method: First, *protect* and *rest* the injured area. Next, *ice* the injured area as soon as possible, use *compression* (apply pressure to the area), and then *elevate* the injury. This will prevent swelling.

2. Expose the injured area to progressively increasing stress as soon as the injury has stabilized. Start with light stretching and build from there.

3. Continue to do the rehabilitation exercises even after the injured limb is as strong as the healthy limb.

On-Water Training

Keeping the fire burning, staying motivated, and maintaining practice intensity can be hard if you do the same thing every day. On-water training drills and games keep you engaged mentally and physically so that training remains rewarding and fun. Athletes who love to practice and relish the process of improvement are destined for greatness. Everyone loves the feeling of winning; athletes who love to train and improve as much as they love to win will win the most. You can be such an athlete by making your training fun, exciting, and challenging.

In his article "Seven Ways to Stir the Coals: Coaching Strategies to Keep the Fire Burning for the Decade It Takes to Build a Champion," Sean McCann suggests a variety of strategies for keeping practice interesting, challenging, and fun. This section presents some of these strategies as well as others and shows you how to adapt them to your water skiing or wakeboarding training.

Make Training a Challenge

People are most motivated and focused when faced with physical or mental challenges that are appropriate for their skill level. A challenge that is too simple quickly becomes boring; one that's too difficult can cause frustration. Your challenge, then, is to find challenges that will keep you interested and motivated. Fortunately, many methods exist for putting yourself to the test and overcoming the boredom of high-volume training. Continually creating challenges in your training is also essential to prevent bad habits from developing. When you get bored and start going through the motions, bad habits and lax technique can creep into your training. These won't be easy to eliminate when you're ready to compete.

To add some spice to your training, ski or ride at different speeds across multiple passes to increase self-awareness, technique control, and energy-pacing skills. Runners use superslow movements to feel each muscle and movement. Do the same on the water. Slow down the boat and give yourself extra time to feel each movement or technique. You can also try new or different techniques to challenge your creativity and experience new positions on the water. One way to increase your creativity, particularly in the off-season, is to ski or ride with your opposite foot forward. This forces you to consciously focus on balance and alignment and will help you develop a more symmetrical body. Another strategy is to do your pass order, trick order, or moves randomly rather than in the sequence you are accustomed to. You can also try your trick run backward or skip slalom passes. The variability keeps you on your toes.

Adjust Your Training Environment

We all like stability and familiarity: same site, same driver, same conditions. A predictable training environment is great when you are making changes in equipment and you want controlled circumstances, but we all need variety in our training environments. Intentionally changing the environment and conditions can improve learning, adaptability, and flexibility.

We all have patterns we may not even recognize, and we often train based on tradition rather than specific need. Make a conscious plan to rotate or change the pattern of your training to keep it fresh, fun, and novel. Even with changes, you can still have a highly structured, scientific training program.

You can shake up training in countless ways. Try switching to morning rather than afternoon practice sessions. It can be a shock to your system, but your mind and body may be fresher, and you may find that you learn better in the morning. Something as simple as having your partner go first or having your partner choose the structure of your set can make practice more fun and challenging. You can also try practicing twice as long one day and then taking a day off rather than having two medium-length training days in a row. Put a new driver at the helm, start at the other end of the lake, or ski or ride at a different lake. Change the setting on the speed control, or start at a different speed or rope length. Try any or all of these strategies and you will not only break up your routine but also learn and document for later what you need to do to ski or ride well in that circumstance. If you face any of these circumstances in competition, you will be confident and do well because you will have a plan and know exactly what to do.

Refresh Your Thinking

Physical preparation is meaningless if you are not also learning mental preparation. When thinking becomes rote, it is often predictable and unproductive. You can change your thinking by changing how you interact with others during practice. A quiet practice session, in which everyone remains silent, forces you to tune in to your own self-talk and focuses your practice. It also helps your coaches and partners become aware of the importance of good communication and positive support during training days.

Defining pretraining goals is another way to stay mentally focused in practice. This is a particular favorite of mine. Before each set I ask myself, What do I want to think about or get done? Having one thing to work on or accomplish on each day or session behind the boat eliminates distraction. That focus on one movement or the number of passes or tricks that you must accomplish also speeds up technical improvements, gears each practice for success, and increases physical and mental awareness. Always have a goal, even if the goal is to do less today than yesterday because you are tired. Even when you are three months away from your next competition and you are in a high-volume, low-intensity, repetitive training phase, have a goal for practice. Make sure it is clear to you and to your partners. This focuses you on the skills you need to develop to be your best.

Visualize New Skills

Many of us are visual learners; we have to see it to believe it. If you see another skier or boarder make a move, try picturing yourself doing it in your head as the first step to learning the new skill. Do more than just see it in your head. Try to feel the movement of the new technique. Understand why it is done a specific way and how to move your body. A technical cue word can anchor that feeling in your mind, and you can use that word to visualize it again and again in practice and in competition. Visualization forces you to focus on what you need to do to execute a skill successfully. In many cases, visualization can actually accelerate learning and reduce frustration.

Practice Coaching Yourself

Getting coaching from others is great, but ultimately, your coaches, training partners, and anyone else who helps you will not be on the water with you. Thus, sometimes figuring out what you are doing right or wrong can be helpful. Learn to describe what happened, rather than relying on others to tell you what they saw. Ask your coach to stop workouts and ask you questions about how you are performing a particular skill. Consider how it felt, observe anything that happened, and consider why you think those things happened. Once you have this awareness of yourself, you can learn to make the necessary adjustments with confidence when your coach is not there. Watching videotapes of your practices is another great way to develop more awareness of the skills you need to concentrate on, and to build the confidence you need to make changes on the fly.

Stop Stinking Thinking

One of the great challenges for every athlete is learning how to stop "stinking thinking," or negative thoughts. We all get tired and frustrated and have bad days, and sometimes we feel that way before competition, too. Learning how to stop negative thoughts and get yourself mentally right is a skill to be mastered. Notice how your own negative comments control your moods and behavior during practice. You can even make it a game by fining your training partners or yourself anytime you say "I can't" or have a bad attitude on the water.

This strategy does not stop at identifying the negativity. Once you are aware of the stinking thinking, you must learn to reverse it or at least neutralize it to a point at which it does not hurt your performance. Sometimes, awareness is enough to get you to straighten out your attitude; other times, you may need help from others to get you in the right frame of mind. Be sure to ask for help when you need it.

Do One Thing Perfectly

Some days, it feels as if you are only going through the motions of practice. You may be thinking about the rest of your life, what you'll have for lunch, or an assignment due for school or work. When this happens, you are no longer in the moment, which affects your performance. One way to bring your mind back to your practice is to try to do one thing perfectly in that day's practice session.

The thing you do perfectly can be anything—a technique, a stretch, a warm-up activity, or a body position on a trick. Whether the perfect thing happens at the beginning, in the middle, or at the end of practice does not matter. The point is to be able to walk away from the session knowing that you cannot do that one thing better than you did it that day. This strategy has multiple effects: You stay alert and make every day of practice worthwhile. It makes you aware that much of your training is far from perfect. It also builds confidence and motivation because you can give yourself credit for good training. This makes even the most mundane practice a time to experience personal excellence.

Have Fun

Practice is not practice when you are having fun. We are all kids at heart, and all kids love games. We all started skiing and riding because it was fun. Don't let the time and effort it takes to be a champion sap the fun out of you. Invent games to make practice fun. With some creativity, you can turn almost any technical skill into a game. You can even make repetitive drills a game by seeing who can do them the best, most, or fastest. Adding a sense of play to your practice settings can generate new enthusiasm and energy, raise intensity, and remind you why you love this sport. Think of kids' games, such as Simon Says, Copy Cat, and Tag, that can be transferred to the water. Of course, when adding games to your training, make sure you are still attentive to using proper movements and skills. Don't focus so much on winning the game that you sacrifice proper technique. Design games with your technical goals in mind, and invent a competitive or noncompetitive game to teach or practice each skill.

Putting Off-Water and On-Water Practice Together

As a skier or rider, you are constantly evolving your skills and abilities. You are learning new movements and feeling and seeing things differently as your skills improve. Over time, things that once seemed difficult become natural. You develop a heightened awareness of what you need to do and how you need to move in various circumstances. As you become more self-reliant, your versatility and adaptability improve as well so that you are prepared for the changing conditions that affect performance. The skills, drills, and games you practice both on and off the water are designed to teach versatility and adaptability so you don't have to think when you are performing. The rule of three states that trying to remember more than three things at once creates overload. Keep it simple by using simple cues or phrases to trigger your three focus points. Mine are *Ski Big, Ski Strong, Ski Confident.* Each phrase creates a mental image of how I want to ski, and the three phrases address both on- and off-water triggers that match my skiing style and preparation.

Fine-tuning your training program and balancing on- and off-water practice is an ever-changing process. If you miss a day of training because of an injury or other commitment, don't fret and don't try to make it up; simply pick things up on the next scheduled day and get after it. Often, people miss one day of training and let it snowball into slacking off. If you have an injury or limited time in which to practice, make a plan for practicing what you can given your limitations. You can still do mental and other elements of training that are not affected by the injury or time constraint. Make the needed changes in your plan and go on, taking one step at a time and enjoying each success on the way to achieving your goal of getting better where it matters most, behind the boat.

Chapter 9

Competing

The ultimate measure of athletic greatness is consistency. From Kris and Bob LaPoint to Rhoni Barton-Bischoff and Regina Jaquess, one element is always the same—a remarkable level of performance consistency under any circumstance. These athletes have developed the special ability to control the process of performing at the top of their capabilities when it matters most.

The majority of this book focuses on how to train in a smart, organized, and scientific manner so you continue to improve your skills and meet your goals. Doing so may make you better, but to perform in competition, you must convert your skills into a competition performance. This chapter will help you do just that by teaching you when to train and when to trust your preparation so you can turn it on when you need to be at your best. When you know how and when to train and how and when to trust and have faith in your training, you free your body to perform the movements you are truly capable of!

Training Mode

In training mode, you should have hypersensitive awareness of a particular facet of your techniques or style that is incorrect and that you are learning to adjust with a new or different movement. The faulty movement could be caused by a fellow skier's comment about your body's strength or structure or any other number of causes. Your own internal instincts and natural balance reactions to an incorrect equipment setup can also cause incorrect movements. In training mode, you must be very cognizant of what you see, feel, and sense on the water and be able to describe it to others to get good coaching feedback. When you are practicing a particular technique, you must be extremely focused on what you are trying to change. You need to learn the difference between what it feels like to do the move right and what it feels like to do it wrong. Every time you perform that movement, your thoughts should be zoned in on this movement so you can feel the change and reproduce the movement consistently.

This next training tip may well be the most valuable in this book. It is based on two tried-and-true coaching and training techniques: using slow motion coordination and using repetition to build retention. You cannot fix technical flaws in competition or when you are pushing yourself to your physical limits. No athlete in any other sport trains this way. It would be like Usain Bolt or Michael Phelps trying to set a world record in every practice session. A better, smarter, and faster way to learn and make changes in technique or movements is to first perform them in slow motion using a long rope at slow boat speeds. You can use training ropes for balance or any other aid to get the feeling, balance, and movement down. Then, do it over and over, letting the repetition build muscle retention. Some of the most difficult movements may require up to eight weeks to change.

When you can do a move every time using a long rope or slow speeds or with whatever help you need, you can move up to more difficult tricks, passes, and speeds. Don't beat your head into the ground. Start slowly and do it right because each incorrect attempt is just one more attempt you will have to correct to rid yourself of a bad habit! After establishing how a new movement looks, feels, and positions, you then start with an easy set and work on repetition and consistency and slowly increase the difficulty. We have all heard the famous Jack Nicklaus quote, "Perfect practice makes perfect."

The next part of the evolution is learning the connection between visual perceptions and physical feelings. This is often best accomplished with video work. Use video to compare your old move to the new one, or watch what you are doing compared to a role model you want to imitate. I vividly remember watching Andy Mapple nail an on-side turn with massive angle across the wakes. I witnessed him compress his knees into his body and rocket the ski out in front of him to dampen the speed and set his edge for his off-side turn. After weeks, maybe months of trying to emulate that move, I finally knew I was close when I felt what Andy looked like when I made a big turn and advanced the ski correctly. When I saw the video of me doing the same movement, I knew I had it down.

In training, you want to be able to compare the feeling of the incorrect technique and the feeling of the correct one. Focus on doing as many repetitions as needed to engrain the feeling of a new move. Video can also help you establish a new feeling in your mind's eye. The key is to make many correct repetitions and not just a bunch of passes!

Trusting Mode

You must know when and how to turn training mode off and trust your preparation. We have all experienced trusting mode from time to time. Some days, something special just happens on the water. Every movement is effortlessly smooth and pure, and you feel perfectly balanced and confident about how the ski moves with your body. You are allowing your body to naturally get you to where you need to be without allowing your mind to tell you how to do it! Trusting mode is having faith that your body knows how to move correctly if you let it work freely. Sometimes, when you are having trouble with a difficult movement or new skill, the problem may be in your mind because you simply cannot think as fast as things happen on the water.

You learn how to ski in trusting mode slowly and in stages. After training and focusing extra hard on changing a movement or learning a new one, there comes a time when you have to trust what you have done in practice. You must allow your body to react in the new manner naturally, which is why paying attention to the new feelings you have on the water during practice is critical. Through proper practice, you move these feelings and manipulations into your subconscious so that you can ride without hundreds of technique thoughts clogging your mind. Repetition builds retention.

Repeat your easy passes or tricks to convert the movement from training to trusting, building your way slowly up to more difficult passes or tricks. If you cannot make the proper movements when it is easy, it will be impossible to make them at more difficult passes or speeds. Start slow, start easy, and build trust and confidence until you are successful in implementing the new move. Falling is only an indication that you need more repetition practice and video study. You cannot expect to have any consistency if your mental checklist includes several hundred things. You must learn to trust your preparation and give it six to eight weeks of consistent practice to make the conversion fully.

The next step is to take your trusting mode to a tournament. In your first tournaments, the goal is to learn, get comfortable, and set yourself up for success in any circumstance. To do so, start at a longer-than-usual rope length or a slower speed in the slalom. If you are trick skiing or wakeboarding, start with some easy tricks, and make sure your first jump has a good landing.

Once you get more into competition and are learning to convert from training to trusting, use your first three slalom passes or tricks to learn and feel how to trust what you have changed. You might find on your first pass or trick that you still have all the mechanical thoughts about what you have been changing. Don't let them distract you. It is part of the process. At the end of that pass, forget the mechanics and start focusing on the second pass and think only about the feeling you want to have. Visualize where you want be on the water and the rhythm you want to have. Take a few deep breaths, and clear your mind. Don't think about anything. Just say "Hit it!" with a free mind and let it happen.

Precompetition Meal

Scientists have researched both the timing and the content of the precompetition meal to a great extent. Their findings have not revealed any one menu that is right for everyone or for every sport. But they all agree that a nutritionally sound precompetition meal will not compensate for poor dietary habits in the weeks leading up to the competition. In fact, research has shown that the food and beverages you consume the weeks before an event do have an impact on performance. However, nutritionists suggest that the psychological benefits of the precompetition meal should not be underestimated. Performance depends on feeling at your peak physically, mentally, and emotionally. The routine and camaraderie of eating well-liked foods with family or friends may give you the needed edge over the competition. Nutritionists do offer this tip: Eat familiar foods and drink plenty of water.

When planning your precompetition meal, first select foods you like and tolerate well. Eat something you are accustomed to eating to prevent gastrointestinal distress such as diarrhea. Don't go off to a tournament and try the local fruit or meal before you compete. Wait until after the competition for that. Your diet should be rich in carbohydrate such as bread and pasta, but low in fat. Drink as much water or juice as comfortably possible to ensure that you are properly hydrated. Dehydration undermines many athletes' performances before they even start their event, so make sure you take plenty of fluids the day of and the days leading up to your competition. If your urine is clear and you are going to the bathroom every two to four hours, you are in good hydrated shape. If you get hungry just before your event or throughout the day, you should eat carbohydrate-rich snacks and keep pumping in the fluids.

You should have your last meal no less than two hours before your event. If nerves keep you from eating a full meal, snacking on a nutritional bar or smoothie can give you the energy you need to compete. This time frame gives you ample time to empty your stomach before the time of competition, yet you won't feel weak or hungry. Timing your food intake is a matter that you must play with to determine what works best for you. The key is to feel strong, fresh, and mentally focused so you are ready to perform at your best. Once you determine a pattern for your digestion and how you feel after a meal, you know the recipe for your perfect precompetition meal.

Precompetition Warm-Up

A strategy many sports greats use to get into the trusting mode for competition is the precompetition warm-up ritual. You can introduce this strategy into your training to get you ready for peak performance consistency. Every great performer has rituals. Some are more obvious and elaborate than others. You have seen them at the free throw line, on the pitcher's mound, in the batter's box, on a serve in tennis, or in a golf swing. These sometimes bizarre mannerisms are sometimes unrelated to the mechanics of the sport or movement, but can become powerful triggers for creating the mental state of peak performance. Rituals help deepen concentration, turn on the automatic pilot, raise intensity, and help you stay loose and in a positive mind-set. These are all things you want in trusting mode.

Rituals help skiers and boarders achieve their ideal performance state (IPS). You can learn to reach your IPS by monitoring yourself and tracking your scores. Record how you feel before, during, and after a competition or practice. By collecting this information, you will begin to see patterns in your performances and be able to relate them to how you felt before the event. Once you know what your IPS is, you can simply recreate or reenact the thoughts and feelings that preceded it. Following are the phases of a precompetition warm-up routine that several national and world champion skiers have used to attain their IPS. Try it out in practice, make adjustments, and then use it in competition. No matter what you do, find a ritual that gets you to your IPS. Doing so will help you become a more consistent peak performer.

- **Phase 1—intensity management.** To warm up, begin by doing 5 to 10 minutes of light aerobic activity (walking, jogging, jumping jacks) to raise your body temperature and dissipate nervous energy. Research has shown that peak performances occur when muscle temperature is slightly elevated while heart rate remains normal, so the next step of the warm-up phase is to bring your heart rate down by doing some stretching (see chapter 2). Be careful not to overstretch because it has been shown to cause the muscles to react slower.

- **Phase 2—mentally rehearsing or visualizing the event.** The awesome power of visualization and mental rehearsal is well documented. Mental imaging is a skill that can be difficult to master and must be practiced. These tips will make the process easier: Sit down in a quiet, comfortable place and relax for several moments. Take three deep breaths, allowing your lungs to fill with air until your stomach extends outward. When your body is relaxed, create a mental movie of the perfect slalom set, jump, or trick run. Try to use as many senses as possible. Feel the water, hear the boat and the fans, smell the air. Mentally rehearse the positive feelings you wish to have, and create detailed and complete mental images, filling in more details as you go. If unrelated thoughts, feelings, and ideas intrude, relax and put them aside by creating a new image for the mental rehearsal. Practice this process two or three times a week if you have never used mental rehearsal before.

○ **Phase 3—attention control.** Quiet your mind as you visualize your ride. Your mind will become focused, turning your attention toward your performance and away from the events of the day. As this focus improves, stop creating the mental imagery. Trust that you have prepared your mind and that the images you have created are complete. Your first priority right now is to quiet your mind by letting go of all thoughts, ideas, and feelings that come to your attention by either committing them to memory or letting them fade into the distance.

○ **Phase 4—focus of energy.** Rid yourself of negative thoughts. If negative thoughts or feeling arise, relax and deal with them. There is no need to panic or worry—negative thoughts pop up in everyone's mind; the trick is how you deal with them. An effective way of eliminating or erasing negative thoughts is visualizing them being eaten up by a garbage truck, writing them on a chalkboard and erasing them, or writing them on a piece of paper and burning it. The key is first to acknowledge the thoughts in a calm state of mind and then remove them in any way that is comfortable.

○ **Phase 5—thought control.** Focus on the present. As your mind becomes clearer, allow your attention to turn toward the reality of the present moment. Focus on your senses. Focus on the loudness of the boat or the soft rhythm of the waves hitting the shore. Notice the colors of the sky and the shade of the water. Feel the texture of the handle in your hand and the coolness of the water. The key to focusing on the present is learning to be attentive to your senses, to the quality of what you are sensing rather than your interpretation of the meaning. As you come off the dock, go trustingly. Trust that you have prepared your mind and body to function at their best. Trust that you can turn off your analytical left brain and give control to your visual right brain. By doing this, you will turn on your built-in "computer" that will guide you to a perfect performance. All you have to do is get out of the way and allow your mind and body to come together as one and function at optimal levels.

Like every valuable skill, you must practice your precompetition warm-up routine and make it part of your competition-day plan. Take more than enough time to prepare prior to your event so you do not rush or skip part of your warm-up. Know how long before your event you need to arrive so you have time to go through your warm-up routine properly. Study the rituals of top skiers and learn from them; they are excellent models. By determining the best plan for you, you can control the controllable and deal with the uncontrollable in a relaxed, positive manner that leads to consistent peak performances.

Competitive Involvement

If you want to become involved in water skiing and wakeboarding at the competitive level, you'll want to join USA Water Ski, the national governing body of organized water skiing in the United States. This organization is responsible for promoting the sport and developing the rules of competition. (See the Rules of the Sport section for more on the rules.) Affiliated with USA Water Ski are the American Water Ski Association (AWSA) for slalom, trick, and jump skiing and USA Wakeboard (USA-WB). American Barefoot Waterski Club (ABC), American Kneeboard Association (AKA), National Collegiate Water Ski Association (NCWSA), National Show Ski Association (NSSA), National Water Ski Racing Association (NWSRA), United States Hydrofoil Association (USHA), and Water Skiers with Disabilities Association (WSDA) are other divisions of USA Water Ski that may interest you.

Once you are a member of USA Water Ski, you need to find a place to compete. Approximately 630 local water ski clubs throughout the United States are affiliated with USA Water Ski. The clubs provide a working base in almost any locale for development of USA Water Ski programs, and are the local organizers for nearly all water ski competitions in the United States. You can find out about events in your area on USA Water Ski's Web site. If you are a first-time competitor, a good place to start is the Grassroots Series section of the Web site. USA Water Ski has done a terrific job recently of making competition fun, easy, and accessible for everyone.

The sport typically breaks down into 11 divisions by age for both men and women. Table 9.1 shows the age divisions. Some of the grassroots events divide competitors according to experience and skill level as well. To make the sport even more interesting, compelling, and fun to track, they now have a ranking system that allows you to see how you stack up to skiers across the nation in your peer group. The system is easy to calculate and follow. All scores at USA WS–sanctioned tournaments class C and above are submitted for inclusion in the USA WS national ranking list. The list ranks skiers based on the average of their top three tournament scores in slalom, tricks, jumping, and overall. Although they do have some penalties for skiers with fewer than three tournament scores, the system is straightforward and allows for competition across age and gender divisions.

TABLE 9.1 AWSA Age Divisions

Division	Age*
Boys 1 and Girls 1	9 years and under
Boys 2 and Girls 2	13 years and under
Boys 3 and Girls 3	17 years and under
Men 1 and Women 1	18-24 years inclusive
Men 2 and Women 2	25-34 years inclusive
Men 3 and Women 3	35-44 years inclusive
Men 4 and Women 4	45-52 years inclusive
Men 5 and Women 5	53-59 years inclusive
Men 6 and Women 6	60-64 years inclusive
Men 7 and Women 7	65-69 years inclusive
Men 8 and Women 8	70-74 years inclusive
Men 9 and Women 9	75-79 years inclusive
Men 10 and Women 10	80-84 years inclusive
Men 11 and Women 11	85 and over
Open Men and Open Women	Any age
Masters Men	35 and over

*A contestant's age on December 31 of the ski year shall determine his or her division for the entire ski year. The "ski year" shall begin on the day after the conclusion of Nationals (held each year in mid-August), and shall end on the final day of Nationals the following year. If a skier's birthday within the ski year could result in an age division change and his or her birthday is between the day after the conclusion of Nationals and December 31 inclusive of that ski year, the skier will ski in the older divisions, beginning the day after Nationals. Otherwise, the skier remains in the younger divisions for one more season concluding with the end of the following Nationals.

From American Water Ski Association, 2010, *Official tournament rules* (Polk City, FL: USA Water Ski), 7. Reprinted with permission from USA Water Ski.

Rules of the Sport

As in all sports, the more you compete, the more you learn the rules of the game. Although there is no substitute for competition experience when it comes to the rules, reading the following rules for each event will give you a head start and help you feel more comfortable before your first event. Slalom and jumping are timed to make sure the boat is going the same speed or the requested speed of the skier. All tournaments and competitions use automatic electronic timers to ensure accuracy. This is one device that is a great convenience for both the skier and driver. It is amazing how far off you can be with hand timing.

Slalom

The object in slalom is to round as many buoys as possible without falling or missing a buoy or gate. The boat travels in a straight path down the center of the course, and the skier makes a serpentine path through the entrance gates around each of the six skier buoys and out through the exit gates. Figure 9.1 gives the dimensions of a slalom course. For information on how to install a course, contact AWSA. Table 9.2 gives the times and tolerances for slalom

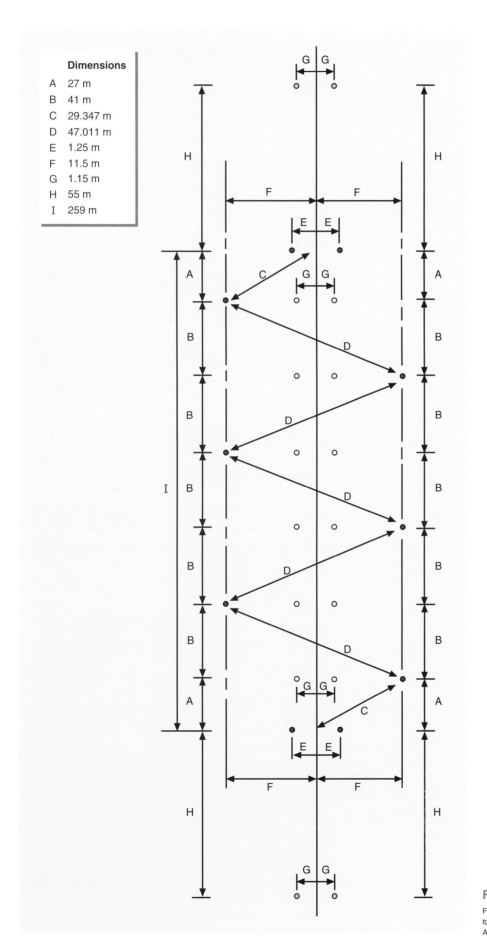

Dimensions

A 27 m
B 41 m
C 29.347 m
D 47.011 m
E 1.25 m
F 11.5 m
G 1.15 m
H 55 m
I 259 m

Figure 9.1 Official slalom course.

From American Water Ski Association, 2010, *Official tournament rules* (Polk City, FL: USA Water Ski), 83. Adapted with permission from USA Water Ski.

TABLE 9.2 Slalom Timing Chart

Boat speed		Score	0-0.5	1-1.5	2-2.5	3-3.5	4-4.5	5-5.5	All 6
km/h	mph	Display	0	1	2	3	4	5	6
58	36.0	Fast	1.64	4.15	6.67	9.20	11.73	14.25	15.92
		Ideal	1.68	4.22	6.77	9.31	11.86	14.40	16.08
		Slow	1.71	4.28	6.84	9.41	11.97	14.53	16.22
55	34.2	Fast	1.73	4.37	7.03	9.69	12.35	15.02	16.78
		Ideal	1.77	4.45	7.13	9.82	12.50	15.19	16.95
		Slow	1.80	4.51	7.23	9.93	12.64	15.34	17.12
52	32.3	Fast	1.83	4.62	7.43	10.24	13.05	15.87	17.72
		Ideal	1.87	4.71	7.55	10.38	13.22	16.06	17.93
		Slow	1.91	4.78	7.65	10.52	13.39	16.25	18.13
49	30.4	Fast	1.94	4.90	7.87	10.85	13.83	16.81	18.78
		Ideal	1.98	5.00	8.01	11.02	14.03	17.04	19.03
		Slow	2.03	5.08	8.13	11.18	14.22	17.27	19.27
46	28.6	Fast	2.06	5.21	8.37	11.54	14.71	17.88	19.98
		Ideal	2.11	5.32	8.53	11.74	14.95	18.16	20.27
		Slow	2.16	5.42	8.68	11.93	15.18	18.42	20.56
43	26.7	Fast	2.20	5.56	8.94	12.33	15.71	19.10	21.34
		Ideal	2.26	5.69	9.13	12.56	15.99	19.42	21.68
		Slow	2.32	5.81	9.30	12.78	16.27	19.75	22.03
40	24.9	Fast	2.36	5.97	9.60	13.23	16.86	20.50	22.89
		Ideal	2.43	6.12	9.81	13.50	17.19	20.88	23.31
		Slow	2.50	6.26	10.02	13.78	17.53	21.27	23.74
37	23.0	Fast	2.54	6.44	10.35	14.27	18.19	22.11	24.70
		Ideal	2.63	6.62	10.61	14.59	18.58	22.57	25.20
		Slow	2.71	6.79	10.86	14.93	18.99	23.06	25.73
34	21.1	Fast	2.76	6.99	11.24	15.49	19.74	23.99	26.81
		Ideal	2.86	7.20	11.54	15.88	20.22	24.56	27.42
		Slow	2.95	7.41	11.85	16.29	20.73	25.16	28.08
31	19.3	Fast	3.02	7.65	12.29	16.93	21.58	26.24	29.31
		Ideal	3.14	7.90	12.66	17.42	22.18	26.94	30.08
		Slow	3.25	8.15	13.05	17.93	22.82	27.70	30.90
28	17.4	Fast	3.33	8.43	13.55	18.68	23.81	28.94	32.33
		Ideal	3.47	8.74	14.01	19.29	24.56	29.83	33.30
		Slow	3.61	9.07	14.51	19.94	25.37	30.80	34.37
25	15.5	Fast	3.71	9.40	15.11	20.83	26.54	32.26	36.04
		Ideal	3.89	9.79	15.70	21.60	27.50	33.41	37.30
		Slow	4.07	10.21	16.34	22.46	28.58	34.68	38.70

From American Water Ski Association, 2010, *Official tournament rules* (Polk City, FL: USA Water Ski), 95. Reprinted with permission from USA Water Ski.

skiing. The score provides the number of buoys a competitor makes it around and the maximum amount of points he or she can receive at that point. At each boat speed, the tolerances show the fastest and slowest times for the boat to move through each section of the course.

Each division has a minimum starting speed and a maximum speed. The skier elects the speed at which to start (only even speeds are allowed) and proceeds to run the course with the speed being increased by two miles per hour after each successful pass. Once the skier reaches the maximum speed for his or her age division, the rope is shortened for the next pass to make it more difficult. The boat stops at the end of the lake and a length of rope (or loop) is taken off. The rope starts at the standard 75-foot (23 m) length, and then is shortened to a 60-foot (18 m) length. This shortening continues until the skier misses a buoy or falls. The lengths are set in preset loops in the rope and are the same for all divisions and tournaments. The loops are located in the increments shown in figure 9.2. Slalom skiers usually refer to the length of the rope based on how much length has been taken off of the full length rope (see table 9.3).

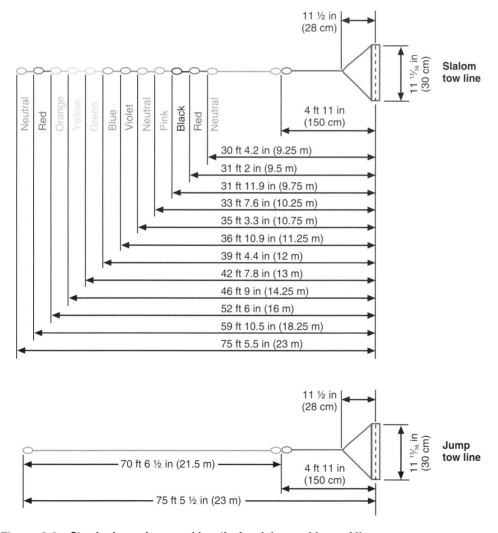

Figure 9.2 **Standard rope loops and lengths for slalom and jump skiing.**

From American Water Ski Association, 2010, *Official tournament rules* (Polk City, FL: USA Water Ski), 82. Adapted with permission from USA Water Ski.

TABLE 9.3 **Slalom Rope Length Names**

Length of rope	Color of last loop removed	Name generally used for this length
75 ft 5.5 in (23 m)	None	Longline
59 ft 10.5 in (18.25 m)	Neutral	15 off
52 ft 6 in (16 m)	Red	22 off
46 ft 9 in (14.25 m)	Orange	28 off
42 ft 7.8 in (13 m)	Yellow	32 off
39 ft 4.4 in (12 m)	Green	35 off
36 ft 10.9 in (11.25 m)	Blue	38 off
35 ft 3.3 in (10.75 m)	Violet	39.5 off
33 ft 7.8 in (10.25 m)	Neutral	41 off
31 ft 11.9 in (9.75 m)	Pink	43 off
31 ft 2 in (9.5 m)	Black	44 off
30 ft 4.2 in (9.25 m)	Red	45 off

Tricks

In a tournament, each skier is given two 20-second passes to perform as many tricks as possible. The 20 seconds begins once the skier passes the optional start buoy and performs the first trick. The first optional start buoy is yellow, which indicates that the skier may start and the clock starts; the second buoy is red and indicates that the clock will begin even if the skier has not started the first trick. The skier gets to select the speed and type of boat and can have a safety release person in the boat. The driver must maintain the chosen speed for the entire course and set the speed control to the skier's preferred settings. Each trick is assigned a point value determined by its difficulty, and the skier who scores the most points is the winner. The trick point values are given in table 9.4.

The best way to develop a trick run that will be successful in competition is to get a pen and paper and make four columns. Write *100%, 80%, 50%,* and *New* as headings for the columns, and enter the tricks you can do that fit into each category. In the *New* column, list tricks that you are working on or want to learn. The real secret to this step is being honest with yourself. Do not overestimate your abilities and put down tricks in the 80% column that you only make 50% of the time on the water. This list forms the foundation of your trick run. How you use it will determine your success.

The next step is to write down the point value (from table 9.4) for each trick on your list. Now, write down last year's trick run and the corresponding point values for each trick. You may be able to simply replace an easy trick with a higher-value trick and gain the points you need to reach your target. An example would be to change a WBB, reverse WBB, WF, WB sequence to WBB, reverse WBB, W5F, WB. This change of one trick would gain you 230 points toward your

TABLE 9.4 Trick Descriptions and Point Values

Description	Water turns				Wake turns			
	Trick no.	Trick code	2 skis	1 ski	Trick no.	Trick code	2 skis	1 ski
Side slide	1	S	20*	40*				
Toehold side slide	2	TS		130*				
180° FB	3	B	30*	60*	14	WB	50*	80*
180° BF	4	F	30*	60*	15	WF	50*	80*
360° FF	5	O	40*	90*	16	WO	110*	150*
360° BB		BB	40*	90*	17	WBB	110*	150*
540° FB		5B	50	110	18	W5B	310*	310*
540° BF		5F	50	110	19	W5F	310*	310*
720° FF		7F	60	130	20	W7F	800*	800*
720° BB		7B	60	130	21	W7B	480*	480*
900° FB					22	W9B	850*	850*
900° BF						W9F	850*	850*
Stepover 180° FB	6	LB	70*	110	23	WLB	110*	160
Stepover 180° BF	7	LF	70*	110	24	WLF	110*	160
Stepover 360° FF					25	WLO	200*	260*
Stepover 360° BB					26	WLBB	200*	260*
Stepover 540° FB					27	WL5B	300*	420*
Double stepover 540° FB						WL5LB		500*
Stepover 720° FF					27A	WL7F	700*	700*
Stepover 900° FB					27B	WL9B	800*	800*
Stepover 540° BF					28	WL5F	300*	420*
Double stepover 540° BF						WL5LF		500*
Stepover 720° BB						WL7B	550*	550*
Stepover 900° BF					28A	WL9F	800*	800*
Toehold 180° FB	8	TB		100*	29	TWB		150*
Toehold 180° BF	9	TF		100*	30	TWF		150*
Toehold 360° FF	10	TO		200*	31	TWO		300*
Toehold 360° BB	11	TBB		200*	32	TWBB		330*
Toehold 540° FB	12	T5B		350*	33	TW5B		500*
Toehold 720° FF		T7F		450	35	TW7F		650*
Toehold 540° BF	13	T5F		350	34	TW5F		500
Toehold 720° BB					36	TW7B		650
Toehold stepover 180° FB					37	TWLB		320

(continued)

TABLE 9.4 *(continued)*

	Water turns				Wake turns			
Description	Trick no.	Trick code	2 skis	1 ski	Trick no.	Trick code	2 skis	1 ski
Toehold stepover 180° BF					38	TWLF		380
Toehold stepover 360° FF					39	TWLO		480*
Toehold stepover 360° BB					40	TWLBB		480*
Toehold stepover 540° FB					41	TWL5B		600*
Toehold stepover 540° LBF					42	TWL5F		700
Toehold stepover 720° LFF					42a	TWL7F		800
Somersault forward					43	FFL	800	800
Somersault backward					44	BFL	500*	500*
Wake double flip					53	DBFL	1,000	1,000
Wake flip back full Twist FF					54	BFLO	800	800*
Wake flip back full Twist BB					56	BFLBB	800	800*
Wake flip back half twist FB					55	BFLB	750*	750*
Wake flip back line back					58	BFLLB	800	800
Wake flip half twist front					57	BFLF	550	550*
Wake flip 540° BF					59	BFL5F	900	850*
Wake flip 540° FB					60	BFL5B	900	900*
Somersault forward with 180 back					61	FFLB	850	850
Somersault forward with 180 front					62	FFLF	850	850
Ski line 180° FB					45	SLB		350*
Ski line 180° BF					46	SLF		400*
Ski line 360° FF					47	SLO		400*
Ski line 360° BB					48	SLBB		450*
Ski line 540° FB					49	SL5B		550*
Ski line 540° BF					50	SL5F		550*
Ski line 720° BB					51	SL7B		750*
Ski line 720° FF					52	SL7F		800*

*Denotes tricks with allowable reverses. Reverses are the same value as basic tricks.

BFL5F and BFL5B must be done hand-to-hand. The rope may not be wrapped around the body to assist the turn. This does not prohibit the simple back position wrap where the rope does not go around the body.

From American Water Ski Association, 2010, *Official tournament rules* (Polk City, FL: USA Water Ski), 91. Reprinted with permission from USA Water Ski.

goal and have no change in sequence or run design. A second strategy is to replace low-point tricks with newly mastered high-point tricks. If you learn a flip and replace a time-consuming sequence such as WB, WF, reverse WF, you gain 180 points and a second or two that can be used for another trick and more

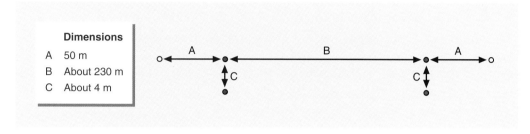

Figure 9.3   A tournament trick course.

From American Water Ski Association, 2010, *Official tournament rules* (Polk City, FL: USA Water Ski), 90. Adapted with permission from USA Water Ski.

points. You should develop a run that is a few hundred points over your target to ensure that you actually reach your goal in competition. Make your run worth 3,200 for a score of 3,000. Figure 9.3 shows a tournament trick course.

Here are a few pointers for putting your run together:

- Always use a trick from your 100% list as your opening trick. Your first trick must be one you are comfortable with and confident about. You have to stand up to score a personal best.

- Position the 80% tricks in spots that allow you to recover from more difficult tricks before attempting the next trick. This can be done by inserting an easy 100% trick such as a BB between a reverse WBB and a W5F. This addition allows you to gather yourself if a problem occurs in the first trick, yet still gains you points.

- Try to link your sequences together using as few positioning tricks (tricks used to put you in position for another trick) as possible.

- Use time management. You get only 20 seconds in a run, which is about enough time for 14 tricks. Don't try to cram an extra four tricks into your run to reach your goal. You may never reach it because if you rush, you may fall.

- Use the 50% tricks as reward tricks. Once you complete a successful run, reward yourself or celebrate by landing a hard trick. Take your time, relax (you can, because you have not included this trick in your run), and nail the trick. View such a trick as a bonus, and soon it will become one of your 80% or 100% tricks.

- Use drills to speed up the learning of new tricks. New tricks are the lifeblood of every tricker. They are the tricks that make a 3,000-point run quickly evolve into a 5,000-point run.

Now that you have done the math and your dream sheet is filled out, it's time to put it to the test on the water. The quickest way to learn a new run is to break it into sections, or sequences, of five or six tricks that go together. B, BB, reverse BB, WBB, reverse WBB, W5F or TO, TB, TF, TS all fit together and should be grouped together for speed and consistency. Practice these sequences slowly and with control until they become comfortable and flow together. Speed is not a concern when you first learn a trick run. Focus on being smooth and consistent; the speed will come once you develop confidence and solid fundamentals.

Jump

The mission of every jumper is the same—to jump the farthest. The one who flies the farthest and skis away is the winner. You get three tries to push your distance out where no one can reach it. The maximum boat speed and ramp height is determined by the division you compete in; however, you can elect to jump on a lower ramp (5-foot, or 1.5 m minimum) or go at a slower speed. You must ride the jump out past the ride-out buoys located at the end of the jump course to get credit for the jump distance. If you are interested in purchasing or building a jump, contact AWSA. Table 9.5 provides the time tolerances for jumping. The record tolerances are used in record tournaments, which are tournaments that are qualified as events in which national or world records can be set. The standard tolerances are used in most other tournaments. The balk times are used when a skier passes the ramp instead of jumping. Figure 9.4 shows a standard jump course.

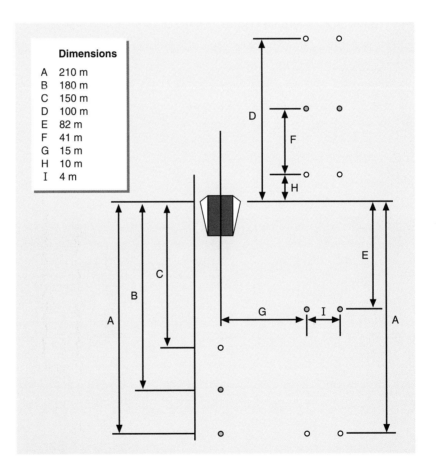

Figure 9.4   Standard jump course.

From American Water Ski Association, 2010, *Official tournament rules* (Polk City, FL: USA Water Ski), 86. Adapted with permission from USA Water Ski.

TABLE 9.5 **Jumping Timing Chart**

	Boat speed		First segment times				Second segment times**		
Record tolerances*	km/h	mph	Balk	Fast	Ideal	Slow	Fast	Ideal	Slow
Apply these tolerance values only when the skier is at the maximum speed for his or her age division.	57	35.4	5.06	5.11	5.18	5.25	2.36	2.40	2.466
	54	33.6	5.34	5.39	5.47	5.55	2.54	2.59	2.66
	51	31.7	5.65	5.70	5.79	5.88	2.68	2.73	2.81
	48	29.8	6.00	6.05	6.15	6.25	2.84	2.89	2.98
	45	28.0	6.40	6.45	6.56	6.68	3.01	3.08	3.17
Standard tolerances*	km/h	mph	Balk	Fast	Ideal	Slow	Fast	Ideal	Slow
Apply these tolerance values at most class C tournaments and in record tournaments when the skier is at speeds lower than the maximum for his or her age division.	57	35.4	5.02	5.07	5.18	5.29	2.36	2.40	2.48
	54	33.6	5.30	5.35	5.47	5.59	2.54	2.59	2.68
	51	31.7	5.60	5.65	5.79	5.93	2.68	2.73	2.84
	48	29.8	5.95	6.00	6.15	6.31	2.84	2.89	3.01
	45	28.0	6.34	6.39	6.56	6.74	3.01	3.08	3.21
	42	26.1	6.78	6.83	7.03	7.24	3.21	3.28	3.43
	39	24.2	7.29	7.34	7.57	7.81	3.43	3.51	3.69

*The tolerance basis for the record tolerances are +/–0.50 mph (+/–0.8 km/h) for the first segment times and +0.62/–0.93 mph (+1/–1.5 km/h) for the second segment times. The tolerance basis for the standard tolerances are +/–0.75 mph (1.21 km/h) for the first segment times and +0.62/–1.24 mph (+1/–2.0 km/h) for the second segment times.

**The second segment boat speed tolerances presume that the boat speed will rise to 3 km/h faster than the baseline speed once the skier is in the air (except 4.5 km/h faster at 57 km/h).

From American Water Ski Association, 2010, *Official tournament rules* (Polk City, FL: USA Water Ski), 94. Adapted with permission from USA Water Ski.

Wakeboarding

To win in wakeboarding, you must not only be able to do the high-point tricks, but also have style and intensity in doing them. There are two primary competition formats. In the first, wakeboarding tricks are assigned point values based on difficulty like in trick skiing, but you are also scored on how well you execute them. You get two 25-second passes to perform five tricks and a wild card trick at the end of the second pass to boost your style points or attempt new tricks that you may have invented in practice.

Wakeboarders focus on getting big air on each of the 10 highest-point tricks they can do, whereas trick skiers move as fast as possible from trick to trick to get more points. Table 9.6 gives the point values and descriptions of some beginning wakeboard tricks and those presented in chapter 5. Table 9.7 provides the descriptions and point values of more advanced tricks that can be performed once you have learned the building block tricks in chapter 5. Use the methodology presented in the trick skiing section to develop your wakeboard trick list.

In the second format, which is used in many pro and international events, each rider gets two passes through the wakeboard course, during which time they may perform any routine they choose. The riders are judged on subjective style categories to arrive at a single combined score.

TABLE 9.6 Point Values of Wakeboard Tricks

Trick name	Point value
Stand on board	20
Ride with one hand on handle	40
Cross one wake	50
Cross both wakes	60
Wave to boat judge	80
Crouch down and touch water	85
Surf the wake	85
Air (one wake)	90
Lip slide	100
Ollie (bunny hop)	125
Surface 180	125
Side slide	130
Surface 360	200
Ollie 180	200
Backside air (two wakes)	200
Half cab	200 (one wake) or 500 (two wakes)
Frontside air (two wakes)	250
Backside air with grab (two wakes)	300
Back scratcher	400
Method	450
Air 180 (two wakes)	450
360 Heli	450 (one wake) or 600 (two wakes)
Stiffy	475
Grab 180	500
Roast beef	500
Indy stiffy	500
Slob heli	650
Backside back roll	1,050
Backside roll-to-revert	1,100
Frontside back roll	1,100
Tantrum	1,200
Backside air raley	1,250
Scarecrow	1,200
Backside mobius	1,500
S-bend	1,600

TABLE 9.7 Additional Wakeboard Tricks

Trick name	Description	Point value
Reverse side slide (touch water)	A side slide with the back toward the boat and the hand touching the water	150
Off the wake 180	The rider uses the boat wake (no air) to change direction	150
Air 180 (one wake)	The rider uses the wake to get into the air and then changes direction	200
Bunny hop 180	The rider changes direction outside the wake by hopping into the air	200
Half cab (one wake)	The rider uses the wake to get into the air and then changes direction	200
Layback	The rider lies back onto the water with the back touching the water	200
Ole	The board rotates 360 degrees on the surface of the water, and the rider performs a handle rotation over the head	250
Off the wake 360	The rider uses the wake (no air) to rotate the board 360 degrees	250
Frontside air with grab (two wakes)	A toe-side air with any grab on the board with either hand	350
Tailbone	Straighten ("bone") out back leg	350
Nosebone	The rider straightens ("bones") out the front leg	400
Bunny hop heli	Outside of the wake, the rider hops and twists 360 degrees	450
Nosebone with tail grab	The rider performs a nosebone and grabs the tail of the board	450
360 heli (one wake)	The rider uses the wake to get into the air and rotates the board 360 degrees	450
Twist	The rider rotates 90 degrees and back	450
Fashion air	A back scratcher with either hand held high and back	450
Melancholy	A front-hand rear heel-side grab	450
Indy bone	A nosebone or tailbone with a toe-side grab between the feet	450
Palmer	A front-hand heel-side grab with a twist	475
Nuclear	A rear-hand heel-side grab with the back leg boned out	475
Double bind half cab	A blindside back-to-front with two hands behind the back approach	500
Crail	A rear-hand front toe-side grab with the back leg boned out	500
Double bind 180	A blindside two-wake 180 with two hands behind the back	500
Rocket air	A tailbone with a two-handed forward grab on the tip	500
Half cab (two wakes)	An air 180, back to front, clearing two wake	500
Canadian bacon	A stiffy with a heel-side grab	525
Switch-stance 360 heli (two wakes)	Starting from the fakie position, the rider uses the wake to get air and rotates 360 degrees (clearing two wakes)	600
360 heli wrap (two wakes)	The rider uses the wake to get air and rotates 360 degrees (clearing two wakes)	600
Tumble turn	The rider goes onto the surface with the back touching and rotates; then returns to normal stance	700
Frontside 360 heli hand pass (two wakes)	Using the toe-side approach, the rider uses the wake to get air, rotates 360 degrees, and passes the handle behind the back from one hand to the other (clearing two wakes)	750

(continued)

TABLE 9.7 *(continued)*

Trick name	Description	Point value
Backside 360 heli hand pass (two wakes)	Using the heel-side approach, the rider uses the wake to get air, rotates 360 degrees, and passes the handle behind the back from one hand to the other (clearing two wakes)	750
FS/BS 540 wrap or hand pass (one wake)	The rider uses the wake to get air and rotates a full 360 plus a half (180)	850
540 with a handle pass (two wakes)	Rider uses wake to get air and rotate a full 360 plus a half (180)	1,050
Backside back roll	A heel-side back roll	1,050
FS/BS 540 wrap or hand pass (two wakes)	The rider uses the wake to get air and rotates a full 360 plus a half (180)	1,050
Blender	A backside roll with a wrap heli	1,075
Switch-stance backside air roll	A fakie-to-fakie back roll without using the wake for air	1,075
Backside air roll	A heel-side back roll without using the wake for air	1,075
Fakie-to-fakie back roll	Switchstance Backside Roll	1,100
Shifty 360	The rider does a twist past 90 degrees; then reverses into a 360-degree rotation in the other direction.	1,100
Switch-stance frontside air roll	A toe-side fakie-to-fakie back roll without using the wake for air	1,125
Frontside air roll	A toe-side back roll without using the wake for air	1,125
Backside air roll-to-revert	A heel-side back roll-to-fakie landing without using the wake for air	1,125
Backside front roll	A heel-side front roll	1,150
Frontside front roll	A toe-side front roll	1,150
Frontside roll-to-revert	A toe-side back roll-to-fakie landing	1,150
Switch stance frontside roll	A fakie-to-fakie back roll	1,150
Backside half cab roll	A heel-side backroll-fakie approach/front landing	1,150
Frontside air roll-to-revert	A toe-side back roll-to-fakie landing without using the wake for air	1,175
Backside air half cab roll	A heel-side backroll-fakie approach/front landing without using the wake for air	1,200
Frontside half cab roll	A toe-side backroll-fakie approach/front landing	1,200
Switch roll blind 180	A heel-side fakie roll-to-front, spinning blind	1,200
Switch-stance tantrum	A fakie tantrum, spinning blind	1,200
Bel air	A tantrum without using the wake for air	1,225
Eggroll	A no-wake scarecrow	1,225
FS/BS 540 hand pass (two wakes)	The same as the two-wake wrap 540, but the handle must exchange hands behind the back	1,250

Trick name	Description	Point value
Frontside air half cab roll	A toe-side backroll-fakie approach/front landing without using the wake for air	1,250
Frontside front flip	Starting toe-side, the rider uses the wake to get air and flips forward, board over head	1,250
Backside front flip	Starting heel-side, the rider uses the wake to get air and flips forward, board over head	1,250
Tootsie roll	A front roll to blindside 180	1,250
Tantrum-to-fakie	A tantrum with a fakie landing	1,250
Backside krypt	A heel-side air raley with a 180-degree turn (landing opposite the direction of the takeoff)	1,250
Switch-stance krypt	A fakie backside raley-to-front landing	1,250
Hoochie glide	An air raley with a method grab (a heel-side grab)	1,250
Switch-stance raley	A fakie backside raley-to-fakie approach/landing	1,250
Air krypt	A toe-side air raley with a 180-degree turn (landing opposite the direction of the takeoff)	1,250
Switch-stance front flip	A front flip with a fakie approach/fakie landing	1,250
Front flip	Starting heel-side or toe-side, rider uses wake to get air and flips forward, board over head	1,275
Front flip-to-fakie	A front flip with a half twist-to-fakie landing	1,300
Frontside air raley	Starting toe-side, the rider goes into the air and raises the board above the body, pushing the board up (inverted)	1,300
Hoochie glide-to-fakie	An air raley with a heel-side grab and a fakie landing	1,300
Shifty 540	The rider does a twist past 90 degrees; then reverses into a 540-degree rotation in the other direction	1,350
Half cab front flip	A front flip with a fakie approach/front landing	1,350
Blind judge	A backside raley to blindside 180	1,350
Hasseloff	A switch-stance front flip to blindside 180	1,400
Whirlybird	A tantrum mobius with an overhead handle pass	1,400
Tweetybird	A no-wake whirlybird	1,425
Frontside tweetybird	A whirlybird starting from a toe-side approach off the wake	1,455
Switch-stance mobius	A two-wake fakie-to-fakie mobius	1,500
Slurpy	Zane Schwenk's signature move.	1,500
Frontside 720 (two wakes)	A heel-side double 360 heli crossing both wakes	1,500
Backside 720 (two wakes)	A heel-side double 360 heli crossing both wakes	1,500
Air switch-stance mobius	A two-wake fakie-to-fakie mobius, not using the wake for air	1,525

(continued)

TABLE 9.7 *(continued)*

Trick name	Description	Point value
Air mobius	A heel-side rotational roll-combination flip with a handle pass *not* using the wake for air	1,525
Skeezer	A switch-stance crow mobe	1,550
Scarecrow mobius	A toe-side front roll-to-revert mobius	1,550
Pete Rose	A toe-side rotational roll-combination flip with a handle pass	1,600
X-mobe	A switch-stance frontside mobius	1,600
Mobe 5	A backside mobius with an extra 180 rotation	1,625
Air mobe 5	A no-wake backside mobius with an extra 180 rotation	1,650
Vulcan	An S-bend to fakie	1,650
Frontside 900 (two wakes)	A toe-side double 360 heli with an additional 180 rotation	1,750
Backside 900 (two wakes)	A heel-side double 360 heli with an additional 180 rotation	1,750
Fat chance	A switch-stance front flip mobius	1,750
Front flip mobius	A heel-side rotation roll combining a front flip with a handle pass	1,750

Chapter 10

A Lifetime of Fun

n their article "Long-Term Athlete Development: Trainability in Childhood and Adolescence," Istvan Balyi and Ann Hamilton describe what researchers call the 10-year or 10,000-hour rule: Talented athletes need 8 to 12 years of training to reach elite performance levels in their sports. The 10,000 hours break down into about three hours of practice every day for 10 years. Most of us can only wish we had three hours a day to train like the pros. Because most recreational athletes don't, they may need a lot more time to reach the peak of their skills. This is great news because it means that you are likely still getting better.

Putting skill progression and learning into this long-term context forces us to reevaluate the idea of peaking for a weekend tournament or any short-term view of training and performance. Rather than emphasizing immediate results, we can refocus our training on a long-term plan for improvement. If you want to get better, continue to have fun, build on your success, and learn to win.

Benefits of Late Specialization

Some sports, such as gymnastics, are young people's games. Gymnastics requires early specialization to reach elite levels. The gymnasts in the Olympics are as young as 14 and 15 and are at the peak of their competitive careers. After college, little or no competitive or recreational opportunities exist. Water skiing and wakeboarding, on the other hand, are late specialization sports, providing lifelong opportunities for skill development and fun. The physical requirements of these sports require you to be more developed physically to perform the movements at the elite level. Thus, water skiers and wakeboarders reach their peaks later in life and are likely to continue to participate for longer periods of time.

Thirteen-year-olds may dominate in gymnastics, but you won't see them jumping 200 feet (61 m) or running 39 off on the slalom course. You will, however, see people 40 years old and older ripping it up on the water and still competing at elite levels. You will also see water skiers and wakeboarders participating in the sports recreationally well past their competitive peaks. This is great news because it most likely means that your best years are ahead of you. I am living proof of this. Although I had been a recreational slalom skier on open water, I did not get on a slalom course until I was 19 years old. Because water skiing is a late specialization sport, I was able to ascend to the top ranks of the sport and have an accomplished pro career spanning three decades of competition.

Six-Stage Model of Development

Water skiing and wakeboarding are sports that provide a lifetime of fun, and they require a specialized model of skill development. Balyi and Hamilton's article presents a six-stage model of development for late specialization sports. I have adapted this model to help water skiers and wakeboarders of all ages map out a lifetime of fun on the water. I have tailored the model to fit our sports skill development and to address the various points at which water ski and wakeboard athletes may begin the process. The model includes the following six stages:

1. Learning to move
2. Learning to train
3. Training for improvement
4. Training to compete
5. Training to win
6. Training for recreation

1. Learning to move

In the learning to move stage, the objective is to learn fundamental movement skills that can be used in any sport. This stage usually occurs around the ages of 6 to 9 for boys and 6 to 8 for girls. This first stage is about learning agility, balance, coordination, and speed (known as the ABC'S of athleticism). Whatever their age, new water skiers and wakeboarders need to learn these skills on the water and behind the boat before they move on to learning the specific skills of edge control, pressure control, rotation, and balance. This approach is vital for young and older skiers and boarders alike, and it will contribute significantly to future achievements on the water. A supportive, highly positive, competence-driven, and fun practice atmosphere can contribute to the successful development of the ABC'S. Use games on and off the water to build speed, power, and endurance, along with the agility, balance, and coordination required behind the boat.

Kids and adults who participate in multiple sports typically progress rapidly through the learning to move stage and experience early success. This develops a sense of competence that motivates and inspires a love for the sport. For this reason, participation in as many sports and events as possible is encouraged. In multievent sports such as ours, event specialization prior to age 15 is not recommended. First, it contributes to athlete burnout, drop-out, and retirement from training and competition. Second, the crossover of skills from multiple events helps to develop balance and strength and the coordination of movement with the motion of the boat.

The first window of adaptation to speed and acceleration typically occurs during this first stage. Speed control and comfort across the wakes, down the lake, and in the turns should be developed in short one- and two-second bursts to build the strength required to stay in control. The agility and quickness developed learning to control speed is vital to learning how to change direction with balance and stability. Again, use games for speed training and keep the volume low (three tries, max) to maintain focus and keep practice from feeling like work.

With four kids at home, I know that keeping up with both kids and adults activities can be a challenge. However, in the learning to move stage, kids should participate in activities that revolve around the school year and summer and winter holidays. Participation in some form of athletics three or four times per week is a key to physical strength development at this stage. If you can't get yourself (or your kids) into other sports, make strength training fun during this stage by doing sit-up, push-up, or pull-up challenges with your friends or with your kids.

In this stage, you need to learn the rules of water skiing and wakeboarding, as well as about safety and manners on the water and in the boat. The skills and knowledge you acquire during the learning to move stage will benefit you in any sport you participate in and lead to a life of more fun and better health.

2. Learning to Train

The objective of the second stage, learning to train, is to learn the fundamental movements of the sport. This stage usually occurs from the ages of 9 to 12 for males and 8 to 11 for females. It applies to skiers and boarders who aspire to improve beyond basic movements behind the boat. Learning to train is about developing the sense of accomplishment and competence that makes water skiing and wakeboarding fun and rewarding.

The preteen years are one of the most important periods for motor development in children; at this time kids' bodies are sometimes growing faster than their coordination can keep up with. This can lead to frustration and damage their sense of competence. This stage also addresses adults who want to improve at the sport they love, but are still developing the strength, balance, and agility required to feel a sense of accomplishment. For these reasons, the specialized movement skills of water skiing and boarding are the focus at this stage. These skills, including tipping, counterrotation, counterbalance, fore–aft balance, and flexing and extending, are the cornerstones of all water skiing and wakeboarding movements. Bypassing learning these skills will slow down learning. Similarly, specialization in one event too early will also inhibit development.

In the learning to train stage, you continue to build overall body strength. Add a medicine ball and a balance ball to concentrate the workout on core abdominal strength along with body-weight exercises and games from the learning to move stage. Put in a few hopping and bounding exercises as well to build some quickness and explosiveness. Endurance games and relays can keep training fun and improve speed, agility, quickness, and change of direction on the water. Introduce basic flexibility during warm-ups.

A 70:30 training-to-competition ratio is recommended with a training plan that fits your school and activity schedule. If you do compete, make it part of the process of improvement and resist the temptation to look at the scoreboard. In tournaments, focus on making the moves you are working on in practice rather than your placement or score.

3. Training for Improvement

The training for improvement stage focuses on building the aerobic engine and consolidating event-specific skills. This stage occurs for males aged 12 to 16 and females aged 11 to 15. It also applies to water skiers and boarders who want to compete. This is the stage at which skiers and boarders find out if they have what it takes. All athletes want to wear the gold medal around their necks or kiss the championship trophy, but not every athlete is willing to train and earn the right to wear that medal or hold that trophy. Training is work; it's hard work if you want to be good and even harder work if you want to be great. If you want to be great, you need to have fun during the process of getting better. You need to love practice and the process of improvement more than the dream of being a champion. With this attitude, the work it takes to be great is not work; you are simply enjoying the process of making progress.

During this stage, athletes start to tie together sport-specific skills and technical tactics. For kids, this is a period of great physical change as their bodies begin to mature. Consequently, a few things need to change in how they train.

Aerobic training becomes a priority to establish a base of fitness. Because of the rapid growth of bones, tendons, ligaments, and muscles, a special emphasis on flexibility training is important to prevent injury. This fitness base is equally important for adults who are new to water skiing and wakeboarding and have not spent time developing the small muscles and flexibility needed for making proper movements and preventing injury.

Plyometrics to build skill, speed, and explosive strength should be introduced along with aerobic and strength training. Base intensity and volume on your physical maturity instead of your chronological age.

A training periodization plan should be developed with attention to your training-to-competition ratio. An overemphasis on competition rather than training during this period in your athletic development can result in a plateau in your career. To prevent this, adjust your training schedule to fit your skills and competitive level, and focus on learning the basics as opposed to competing. Too many competitions distract from valuable training time and slow down the development of technical skills. You will need to learn how to cope with the tactical, physical, and mental challenges presented during competition, but this comes at a later stage. At the training for improvement stage, you want to remain focused on consistent progress and accomplishment.

The recommended training-to-competition ratio during the training for improvement stage is 60:40. The 40 percent of time spent on competition includes competition and competition-specific training in the form of practice matches and competitive games and drills.

4. Training to Compete

Only after the objectives of the training for improvement stage have been achieved do you begin to train to compete. In the training to compete stage, water skiers and wakeboarders should optimize their fitness preparation and sport-specific skills and focus on their performance. This stage takes place around ages 16 to 18 for males and 15 to 17 for females. It is also appropriate for adults who are actively competing.

The training-to-competition ratio at this stage is 50:50—half of the time is devoted to technical and tactical skills and fitness improvements, and the other half is devoted to competition and competition-specific training. Mental intensity increases to correspond with the increases in competition-specific training. At this stage you need to develop and perfect routines and rituals along with other mental toughness skills.

Individual event training on and off the water is done year-round within a periodized schedule. The fundamental sport-specific movements and skills need to be performed under the stress of competitive conditions during this stage. Simulation training for competition, in which you mimic competitive environments and conditions, is a critical part of competition preparation.

Your fitness program during this stage should also include recovery to keep you physically strong. Psychological preparation and competitive toughness along with technical development teach you how to make adjustments mentally, physically, and technically to the circumstances of competition. Your strengths and weaknesses determine your training schedule. With more competition, you may need a double or multiple periodization framework.

5. Training to Win

In the training to win stage, the objective is to maximize fitness and sport-specific skills as well as performance. This stage occurs in males 18 years and older and in females 17 years and older. If there is one stage that is most needed by the overwhelming majority of water skiers and wakeboarders, it is training to win. It is definitely the most overlooked stage in our sports. Many compete, but few win, and even fewer learn how to win consistently.

This stage is the final frontier of skill development; in this stage you learn how to consistently and predictably perform your best, how to turn it on when it matters and make it happen. Training to win is about peaking for major competitions as well as knowing how to adjust, adapt, and dominate the competition even when everything is not set up for a peak or you are not at your best.

The training-to-competition ratio in this phase is 25:75, with the competition percentage including competition-specific training activities. Training to win mostly involves trial and error and testing precompetition routines and practice rituals. It takes great attention to detail and precise tracking to find the consistently reproducible mix of training, warm-up, intensity, focus, and mental calmness so you can ski or ride your best.

In this stage, you need to keep and analyze a detailed log of everything to find patterns of performance in both practice and competition. Think of all the statistics used in golf—driving percentage, greens in regulation, putts made and missed. The same is true of tennis—winners, unforced errors, serving percentage. Track your stats and know what your go-to moves are to win. Likewise, have a plan for situations that force you away from your strengths. So much of learning to win consistently is simply putting yourself in situations you know how to manage and having a plan to execute your skills. A plan helps you eliminate self-doubt and second-guessing and focus on execution. Following a plan, rather than leaving your performance to chance, gives you the best chance of winning.

6. Training for Recreation

In training for recreation, the objective is to continue to compete or to transition into the role of coach, official, or other position. This stage is why water skiing and wakeboarding are sports for a lifetime. At the highest level, years after top athletes have retired from professional competition, they still are actively involved in age group or masters competitions or coaching and officiating. Recreational skiers and boarders can continue to improve and build their skills on the water following the same six steps, adjusted for their skills, ability, and age.

Great athletes constantly are evolving to stay ahead of the competition. Michael Jordan added a fall-away jumper and a three-point shot as he progressed in age and his ability to blow by defenders diminished. As he aged, Muhammad Ali learned that he could bully smaller fighters and took punches to wear down his stronger opponents in pursuit of victory. Michael Phelps began an overhaul of his stroke almost as soon as he returned from the Beijing Olympics so he could get faster. In each case, the athlete had a plan and a process that resulted in consistent improvement and winning. Now you too have a plan and a process. Chart your course to victory.

Note: The italicized *t* and *f* following page numbers refer to tables and figures, respectively.

ABOUT THE AUTHOR

Ben Favret has won championships at every level in his 25 years of competitive slalom water skiing. He has established himself as one of the world's most-respected and best-known competitors by winning gold medals in multiple regional, national, Pan American, world, and professional competitions. He is also the current U.S. men's masters record holder and ranked number 1 in the world by the IWSF 35-45 age division.

Over the years, Favret has coached and trained numerous skiers to victory as the top slalom instructor at Bennett's Water Ski School and now at his own private site in Orlando, Florida. He was the lead author of Human Kinetics' *The Complete Guide to Water Skiing,* which is considered by many to be the bible of water skiing. He has also written over 30 articles in top water ski publications, conducted numerous equipment tests and evaluations, and served on the United States Olympic Committee Athlete Advisory Council and as a board member of USA Water Skiing.

Favret graduated from the University of Alabama with a degree in marketing. He resides in Windermere, Florida, with his wife and four children.

You'll find other outstanding outdoor sports resources at

www.HumanKinetics.com/outdoorsports

In the U.S. call 1-800-747-4457

Australia 08 8372 0999 • Canada 1-800-465-7301
Europe +44 (0) 113 255 5665 • New Zealand 0800 222 062

 HUMAN KINETICS
The Premier Publisher for Sports & Fitness
P.O. Box 5076 • Champaign, IL 61825-5076 USA

 **eBook**
available at
HumanKinetics.com